द्राम् – *Drām*

Śrī Dattātreyar – Ādi Guru

*

Kamalātmānanda Nāthaḥ @ **Dr. Ramamurthy N.**

M.Sc., B.G.L., CAIIB, CCP, DSADP, CISA, PMP, CGBL, Ph.D.

*

*

Name: *Śrī Dattātreyar – Ādi Guru*

First Edition: 2025

Author: *Kamalātmānanda Nāthaḥ* @
Dr. Ramamurthy N,
http://ramamurthy.jaagruti.co.in/

ISBN (13): 978-93-342-7849-1

Number of pages: 157

Price: ₹ 300.00

Printed at:

Published by:

*****

Table of Contents

Dedication 4

Blessings 5

Introduction 7

Ādi Guru Dattātreya 12

Śrī Dattātreya in *Purāṇa*-s 15

Different Forms of *Sri Dattatreya* 23

Śrī Dattātreya Yantra 40

Śrī Dattātreya Mantras 44

Ādi Guru Śiva Datta Nāma Puja 47

Śrī Dattātreya Stotram 50

Śrī Dattātreya Aṣṭa Cakrabīja Stotram 53

Śrī Dattātreya Dvādaśa Nāma Stotram 58

Śrī Dattātreya Vajra Kavacam 60

Śrī Dattātreya Aṣṭottara Śata Nāmāvalī 78

Śrīmad Dattātreya Sahasranāma Stotram 84

Śrīmad Dattātreya Sahasra Nāmāvalī 112

About the Author 154

*****

Dedication

Oṃ Dattātreya Hare Kṛṣṇa Unmattānanda Dāyakā ।
Digaṃbara Mune Bāla Piśāca Jñāna Sāgara ॥

ॐ दत्तात्रेय हरे कृष्ण उन्मत्तानन्ददायका ।
दिगंबर मुने बाल पिशाच ज्ञानसागर॥

This book is dedicated with devotion to all Swamijis who follow the *Avadhoota* Sanyasa system known as *Turiyatītam*. Especially to my *Srividya Guru Pūjyaśrī Pranavananda Brahmendra Saraswati Paramahamsa Parivrājaka Avadūta Mahāswāmi* and to that lineage of Gurus. There is no doubt that they will bestow their blessings upon all of us.

Kamalātmānanda Nāthaḥ @ Dr. Ramamurthy N

Parāpara Guru
Śrī Śrī Judge Swamijī

Parameşţi Guru
Śrī Śrī Swayamprakasha Swamijī

Parama Guru
Śrī Śrī Śāntānanda Swamijī

Guru
Śrī Śrī Pranavānunda Swamijī

*****

உ
ப்ரஹ்மைவ ஸத்யம்
SRI SWAYAMPRAKASA AVADHUTHA SADASIVA TRUST
Sri Sri Judge Swamigal Adhishtanam, East 7th Street,
PUDUKKOTTAI-622 001
Phone: 04322-221440, 222128
Email: sribhuvaneshwari@gmail.com

Blessings

Dattātreya Hare Kṛṣṇa Unmattānanda Dāyakā ।
Digaṃbara Mune Bāla Piśāca Jñāna Sāgara ॥

We are very happy to know that our beloved disciple Dr. Sri. Ramamurthy is going to write and publish a book on *Adi Guru Dattatreya*.

The word *Dattatreya* means, one who has dedicated himself. *Dattatreya* is called the Guru of all Gurus because he was the foremost Guru of divine wisdom. Therefore, he is praised as the "*Ādi Guru*". Lord Dattatreya appears again and again in many forms to uplift his devotees.

There are many stories that show that the Lord manifested Himself in various forms, watching over and protecting His devotees, according to the conditions and merits of the devotees.

Our Pudukkottai Guru lineage is an *Avadhootha* lineage. The *Avadhoota* tradition begins with *Dattatreya*! It is also worth mentioning that there is a Guru Parampara Stotra starting as "*Dattātreya Samārambām*".

King Yadu, the grandson of King Nakush of the Chandra dynasty and son of Yayati, one day met a young Avadhoota monk who had completely renounced his life, how did you acquire such profound and clear wisdom without doing any work? When asked how you, a man of great intellect, can wander in the world happily like a child. The Avadhoot, Dattatreya, describes from whom and what knowledge (spiritual knowledge) he obtained. That is the Avadhoota Gita!

Dattatreya is called a god and an aspect of the Trinity. At the same time, *Dattatreya* is called a guru and the head of the Sannyasa tradition. They call Datta a Yogi and the wisest of all wise men.

But he performs leelas (games) sometimes as a boy, sometimes as an insane and sometimes as a siddha.

The worship of Sri Datta is very popular in the northern parts of India. The first temple dedicated to Dattatreya in Tamil Nadu was built at Senthamangalam. It was built by our Paramaguru, Swayam Prakasha Brahmendra Saraswati Maha Swami, who was popularly known as Senthamangalam Periyava.

I am very happy that Sri Ramamurthy has brought out a book about such a great *Adi-guru*!

May the Guru grace, the author of this book and the devotees who read it. We pray to Goddess Jaganmata Sri Bhuvaneshwari Devi and Sadguru Sri Shantananda Mahaswami to bless with their blessings to attain a blissful and happy life.

Jai Guru Datta! *Sri Guru Datta*!

Āṉandam Śupam Maṅgaḷam I *Jay Buvaṉēśvari I*

Śrī Buvaṉēśvari Pīṭam,
16-04-2025

Śrī Praṇavānanta Svāmiṉaḥ
Pudukkottai

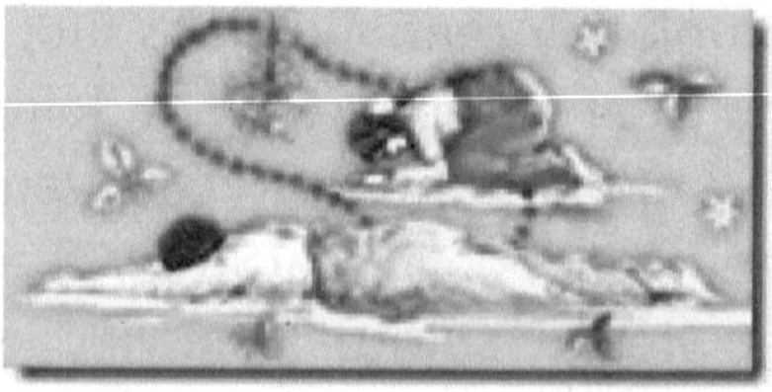

*****

Introduction

Oṃ Śrī Gurubhyo Namaḥ ॥ ॐ श्री गुरुभ्यो नमः ॥

Oṃ Āṃ Hrīṃ Kroṃ Ehi Dattātreya Svāhā ॥

ॐ आं ह्रीं क्रों एहि दत्तात्रेय स्वाहा ॥

Oṃ Śrī Gurudeva Datta.

The force of *Parabrahmam*, without any image, qualities and undefined, which includes a number of morphological, incomprehensible and inexhaustible materials, seems to be limited. The absolute philosophical paradigm is not amorphous.

However, we are not yet mature enough to realise the formless *Parabrahmam* (no need of writing/ reading this book, if we are that much mature). Someone has to hold back or attach side wheels until one learns to drive a bicycle. Once he becomes expert these are not needed. We need a boat to cross a river. Once we have reached the other shore, what is the need of a boat.

Therefore, until we mature, we will try to learn about a God.

In Hindu cosmology, one Jagadguru is born and associated with each of the four *yugas* (Satya, Treta, Dvapara, and Kali) as a prominent spiritual leader to teach and guide us in a proper path;

ॐ कृते तु भगवान् सत्यः, त्रेतायां दत्त एव च,
द्वापरे भगवान् व्यासः, कलौ श्री शङ्कर स्वयम् ।

Oṃ Kṛtetu Bhagavān Satyaḥ, Tretāyāṃ Datta Eva Ca,
Dvāpare Bhagavān Vyāsaḥ, Kalau Śrī Śaṅkara Svayam ।

1. Lord Satyadev (Lord Brahma or Dakshina Murthi) for Satya Yuga
2. Lord Dattatreya for Treta Yuga,
3. Veda Vyasa for Dvapara Yuga, and
4. Adi Shankaracharya for Kali Yuga.

- Satya Yuga – This is also called as Kruta Yuga – This is the golden age, characterized by truth and righteousness. The associated Jagadguru is Lord Satyadev, representing the embodiment of divine knowledge and wisdom. Lord Brahma or Dakshina Murthy is called Satyadev.

Krutayuga Jagadguru Sri Satyadev	Tretayuga Jagadguru Sri Dattatreyar

Dvapara Yuga Jagadguru Sri Veda Vyasa	Kaliyuga Jagadguru Sri Adi Shanara

- Treta Yuga – This yuga is marked by a decline in spiritual purity compared to Satya Yuga. The Jagadguru is Lord Dattatreya, known for his role in guiding humanity towards spiritual progress.
- Dvapara Yuga – This is the age of duality and conflict, where dharma (righteousness) is fading. The Jagadguru is Veda Vyasa, who is credited with compiling all the Vedas and writing other important scriptures.

- Kali Yuga – This is the current age, characterized by decline and materialism. The Jagadguru is Adi Shankaracharya, whose teachings and philosophy are seen as a guide for spiritual seekers in this era.

Śrī Ādi Śaṅkara Bhagwat Pādar, the greatest philosopher and thinker, in a short life span of 32 years, has created a collection of art-essays of Indian culture and the intellectual and emotional integration of this sub-continent.

The supreme beauty of his teachings is that they apply to all human beings irrespective of religion or race, caste or creed or nationality. That is why he is undoubtedly *'Jagadguru'*.

The four ashramas, or stages of life in Hinduism, are Brahmacharya (student), Grihastha (house holder), Vanaprastha (forest dweller/ hermit) and Sannyasa (renunciate).

- Brahmacarya (Student Stage) – This stage focuses on learning and spiritual discipline, often involving celibacy and studying under a guru.
- Gruhastha (Householder Stage) – This stage is characterised by establishing a family, pursuing a livelihood and fulfilling societal duties. It is the moral duty of Grihastha's to feed the Brahmacaries and Sannyasins.
- Vanaprastha (Hermit Stage) – As individuals age, they transition to this stage, often involving a move to the forest or a more secluded life, focusing on spiritual contemplation and detachment from worldly affairs.
- Sannyasa (Renunciate Stage) – In this final stage, individuals renounce worldly attachments and dedicate themselves entirely to spiritual pursuits and seeking liberation (moksha).

These general divisions are represented by various subdivisions, different philosophies, philosophical schools and traditions. The philosophy is a necessity as far as the Bharat Sanatana Dharma is concerned. For others, it is an entertainment (philosophy is a pastime).

Within the above Sannyasa Ashram[1], there are four stages or kinds *Kuṭīcaka, Bahūdaka, Haṃsa* and *Parama-Haṃsa*.

Above all these, there is one highest level called *Turīyātītam* or *Avadhūtam* to attain *Aatmānubhava* (Soul Experience). Such type of Sanyasis renunciate even their clothes and move as *Digambaras*. The foremost (Adi Guru) among such Sanyasis is Sri Dattatreya.

While there are many books on Adi Shankaracharya, not many details are available about Sri Dattatreya. Hence this book aims to be provided comprehensive details about Sri Dattatreya, Adi Guru alongwith his storas and all. A separate book is being written to provide Bhashyam for Dattatreya sahasranama. The following storas/ mantras are covered in this book;

- *Śrī Dattātreya Yantra*
- *Śrī Dattātreya Mantras*
- *Ādi Guru Śiva Datta Nāma Puja*
- *Śrī Dattātreya Stotram*
- *Śrī Dattātreya Aṣṭa Cakrabīja Stotram*
- *Śrī Dattātreya Dvādaśa Nāma Stotram*
- *Śrī Dattātreya Vajra Kavacam*
- *Śrī Dattātreya Aṣṭottara Śata Nāmāvalī*
- *Śrīmad Dattātreya Sahasranāma Stotram*
- *Śrīmad Dattātreya Sahasra Nāmāvalī*

Writing meanings and comments for Samskruta verses is not an easy task. The meaning and beauty of the source should not be fragmented but the clarity of the words should captivate the mind of the readers. The readers should dissolve and melt in the mind of the author of the source. The comments should be written in such a way that the readers can enjoy the sweet juice in it.

Conventions – Wherever **She** is used, it indicates *Sri Devi.* The transliterated Samskrutam or other language words are written in *italics*. When Samskruta words are transliterated in English diacritical marks are used for proper pronunciation like;

---

[1] A separate book explaining the Hindu Sanyasa methods, stages, etc., has been written by the same author in English and Tamil.

ā – as in *Rama* *ḍ* – as in mud
ḍh – as in godhood *ḥ* – visarga in as in *Rāmaḥ*
ī – as in peel *ṇ* – as in pun
ṛ – as in strewn *ś* – as in Shankar
ṣ – as in fish *ṭ* – as in cut
ṭh – as in anthill *ū* – as in root

Humble pranams to HH *ŚrīŚrī* ***Prnavānanda Swāmijee***, who has blessed me and the readers with his nice introduction and some pleasantries. I am fortunate to have association with people like ***Swāmijīs***, who are my *Gurus*. Sincere thanks are due to all who helped me in bringing this book so nicely. It is only because of the blessings of such gurus that I am able to continue my efforts to write books. It is because of their kindness that this 103rd book has been written. I pray at the feet of the gurus to continue such efforts.

Appreciation and acknowledgements are due to all those who supported in this noble cause. The readers are requested to feel free in providing feedback. Let all the readers be blessed with glory of Gods.

With the splendid blessings of our forefathers, priests and Sri Devi, this 103rd book has been completed. My humble salutations to all of them. May their blessings continue.

This book is also being written by the same author in Tamil simultaneously.

Om Tat Sat

Chennai
2025

Dr. *Ramamurthy N*

*****

Ādi Guru Dattātreya

The great task of the Satgurus is to guide men to follow the precepts of the Vedas in every stage of human life, whether it be Brahmacaryam, Grihastha, Vana-Pratham or Sannyasa and ultimately to make him attain the true goal of life, the liberation of the union of the soul and Brahmam. This is the great Guru philosophy that the scriptures say, "*Na Guroradhikaṃ Tatvam* – न गुरोरधिकं तत्वम्" – to show this Guru philosophy to the world and to guide the human society on the right path to those who will incarnate as Satgurus, to show the great masters and the characteristics of a perfect Satguru, the Supreme Being, the embodiment of Sat-Chit-Ananda, decided to incarnate as a Gnana Avatar.

The great ascetic, Atri Maharishi, was engaged in severe penance on the Rishyamukha mountain. The great sage Atri, who conquered the three evil qualities of lust, anger and greed – he was free from all the three evils – that is why he is called *A-tri*. His wife was such a perfect match Anasuya Devi.

Asuya means jealousy towards others. *Anasuya* is the one who is completely free from jealousy, envy and malice. She is an ascetic. She is the daughter of Devahuti and the Prajapati Kardama. In Ramayana, she lives with her husband in a small hermitage on the southern border of the Chitrakuta forest. When Sita and Rama visit her during their exile, Anasuya was very attentive to them. She gave Sita, an unguent that would maintain her beauty forever and other jewels also.

She is a pious woman who leads an austere life, she is described as having miraculous powers. Anasuya is the sister of the sage Kapila, who also served as her teacher. She is extolled as Sati Anasuya (Ascetic Anasuya) and Mata Anasuya (Mother Anasuya), the chaste wife of Sage Atri.

Pleased with sage Atri Maharishi's penance, the three deities asked him what boon he wanted – he prayed to the three deities to grant him a perfect son. For a great sage like Atri Maharishi and for a great devotee like Anasuya Devi, how can one bestow a perfect son other than a child who is filled with the complete attributes of the Trinity?

Therefore, as a sign that the Trinity had given themselves to him. They incarnated bearing the divine name of "*Datta* + *Ātreya* – दत्त + आत्रेय" – *Sri Dattātreya*. We all know the story of Anasuya Devi transforming the three deities into a child and fed the baby, to show the power and glory of her devotion to the entire world.

The philosophy of the incarnation of the *Ādiguru*, Lord *Sri Dattatreya*, is that when the evil qualities of jealousy and hatred are eliminated (*Ànasuya*) + high penance (*Atri Maharishi*) are combined, the state of liberation called *Brahma Sākşādkaram* is attained. Many women in the world have become mothers to Brahma, Vishnu and all, through their penance. But Anusuya Devi only had the great gift of being the mother of all the three deities.

Along with the three faces of the Trinity, Brahma + Vishnu + Maheshwaran, Lord Sri Dattatreya makes us realise that the source of the threefold process of creation + state + samhara is one and the same.

Each weapon that Lord Sri Dattatreya holds in his six hands teaches us higher principles. The aspect of Brahma holds the Akshamala (garland of beads) and the Kamandalu (water pot) in his hands. The Akshamala represents penance and the Kamandalu represents the nectar of knowledge, the fruit of penance.

The conch and the discus, which are the two hands of Lord Sri Maha Vishnu, radiate light. The basis of the universe is the Vedas – the basis of the Vedas is Pranava (*Oṃ*). The conch has its origin the sound Brahmam, the Pranavam. The wheel, which is the shape of the wheel of time, which is without destruction and change, also signifies that the Guru is the Supreme Brahmam.

The trident, the weapon that destroys the ego of '*I*' and the three gunas that are its basis, is used in the delusion of ignorance. The drum called *Damarugam*, which awakens the souls lying in deep sleep with its sound, also shines in the two hands, which are the aspects of Parameshwara.

Sri Maha Periyava About Sri Dattatreya
(Voice of God – Part – 7 – Guru-Disciple-relationship)

Dattatreya is very great. Guru in Vedanta. Guru in Sri Vidya Sampradaya. Guru of Yoga Siddhas as well. He is in the form of Trimurti.

Dattatreya is one of the early pioneers of our Advaita philosophy. In the tower of Acharya Sannidhi in the Kamakshi Ambal Temple, Kanchipuram, there are images of all those who came in the previous acharya lineage. Above all, at the top, our Guru Parampara, Dakshina Murthy image is not placed. The Narayana image that begins the verse with "*Narayanam Padmaphuvam*" is also in the lower row. The image at the top is Dattatreya. His word has great weight.

Many great souls received teachings from Adi guru Datta, who was a great sage and a great yogi and became his disciples. The most prominent among them are Parashurama, Prahlada, Karta Veeryarjuna, Sri Karthikeya and Sage Sankruti.
Audumbara tree which is the favourite of Lord Dattatreya is used for the Deeksha.

Similar to Hanuman, Vibheeshana, Markandeyar and all, Lord Dattatreya is also a *chirancheevi* (eternally living).

Let us try to understand something more about such an earliest Guru and some of his hymns.

*****

***Śrī Dattātreya* in *Purāṇa*-s**

Shrimad Bhagavatam (1.3.11) says Lord Vishnu had his sixth incarnation[2] as Dattatreya to the sage Atri and his wife Anasuya. He is considered as a partial representation of Lord Vishnu and a combined form of the trinity Gods, Brahma, Vishnu, and Shiva. Dattatreya is said to have descended to Earth on the Purnima (Full Moon) day in the Margashirsha month (December-January) of the Hindu calendar. That day every year is celebrated as Dattatreya Jayanthi by all. In some places, Dattatreya Jayanti is celebrated on the Dashami Tithi of the month of Vaikasi (May-June).

In Shrimad Narayaneeyam, 36th Dasakam, 1st verse says – Long ago Thou were born as Dattatreya to the sage Atri and Anasooyaa. Mentally tired by the pesterings of Thy various disciples, Thou wandered about immersed in blissful peace. Thus Thou were seen by the great devotee Kaartaviryaarjuna, the king of Hehaya. Pleased, Thou bestowed on him all psychic powers consisting of the eight Sidhis and also promised him death at Thy hands in the end.

He is often depicted with three faces (representing Brahma, Vishnu, and Shiva) and six hands, symbolizing the combined nature of the Trimurti. Dattatreya is revered for his wisdom, self-realisation and his ability to guide seekers on the spiritual path and hence He is revered as the Adi Guru, a very ancient teacher, and his worship is said to bless with supreme knowledge, sound intelligence, and divine wisdom.

Dattatreya is known for his teachings and is considered the ultimate guru, (Adi Guru – the earliest teacher). Ironically, he says in Shrimad Bhagavatam as he has 24 Gurus. with the story of his 24 gurus being recounted in the Shrimad Bhagavatam (11.9.32) as below;

Once, while Dattatreya was roaming in a forest happily, he met King Yadu, who on seeing Dattatreya so happy, asked him the secret of his happiness and the name of his Guru. Dattatreya said that the

---

[2] Normally we are aware of 10 main incarnations of Lord Vishnu. But Bhagavatam describes 24 incarnations of Lord Vishnu.

Atman alone was his Guru and yet, he had learned wisdom from 24 individuals, who were therefore, his Gurus.

My 24 gurus are – 1. Earth, 2. Water, 3. Air, 4. Fire, 5. Sky, 6. Moon, 7. Sun, 8. Pigeon, 9. Python, 10. Ocean, 11. Moth, 12. Bee, 13. Honey-gatherer, 14. Elephant, 15. Deer, 16. Fish, 17. Dancing-girl Pingala, 18. Raven, 19. Child, 20. Maiden, 21.Serpent, 22. An arrow-maker, 23. Spider and 24. Beetle.

1. I learnt patience and doing good to others from the Earth, for it endures every injury man commits on its surface, and yet it does him good by producing crops, trees, etc.
2. From Water I learnt the quality of purity. Just as the pure water cleanses others, so also the sage, who is pure and free from selfishness, lust, egoism, anger, greed, etc., purifies all who come in contact with him.
3. Air though moving everywhere, never gets attached to anything; so, I have learnt from the air to be without attachment, though I move with many people in this world.
4. Just as Fire burns bright, so also the sage should be glowing with the splendor of his knowledge and Tapas.
5. The air, the stars, the clouds, etc., are all contained in the Sky, but the sky does not come in contact with any of them. I have learnt from the sky that the Atman or the Soul is all-pervading, and yet it has no contact with any object.
6. The Moon is in itself always complete, but appears to decrease or increase on account of the varying shadow of the earth upon the moon. I have learnt from this that the Atman is always perfect and changeless, and that it is only the Upadhis or limiting adjuncts that cast shadows upon it.
7. Just as the Sun, reflected in various pots of water, appears as so many different reflections, so also Brahman appears different because of the Upadhis (afflictions) caused by the reflection through the mind. This is the lesson I learnt from the sun.
8. I once saw a fowler spread a net and caught some Pigeons. The mother pigeon was very much attached to her children. She did not care to live, so she fell into the net and was caught. The male pigeon was attached to the female pigeon, so he also fell into the net and was caught. From this I learnt that attachment is the cause of bondage.

9. The Python does not move about for its food. It remains contented with whatever it gets and lies in one place. From this I learnt to be unmindful of food and to be contented with whatever I get to eat (Ajagara Vritti).
10. Just as the Ocean remains unmoved even though hundreds of rivers fall into it, so also the wise man should remain unmoved among all sorts of temptations, difficulties and troubles. This is the lesson I learnt from the ocean.
11. Just as the Moth, being enamored of the brilliance of the fire, falls into it and is burnt, so also, a passionate man who falls in love with a beautiful girl comes to grief. To control the sense of sight and to fix the mind on the Self, is the lesson I learnt from the moth.
12. Just as the Black Bee sucks the honey from different flowers and does not suck it only from one flower, so also, I take only a little food from one house and a little from another house and thus appease my hunger (Madhukari Bhiksha or Madhukari Vritti). I am not a burden on the householder.
13. Bees collect honey with great trouble, but a Honey-Gatherer comes and takes the honey easily. Even so, people hoard up wealth and other things with great difficulty, but they have to leave them all at once and depart when the Lord of Death takes hold of them. From this I have learnt the lesson that it is useless to hoard things.
14. The male elephant, blinded by lust, falls into a pit covered over with grass, even at the sight of a paper-made female elephant. It gets caught, enchained and tortured by the goad. Even so, passionate men fall in the traps of women and come to grief. Therefore, one should destroy lust. This is the lesson I have learnt from the elephant.
15. The deer is enticed and trapped by the hunter through its love of music. Even so, a man is attracted by the music of women of loose character and brought to destruction. One should never listen to lewd songs. This is the lesson I learnt from the deer.
16. Just as a fish that is covetous of food falls an easy victim to the bait, so also, the man who is greedy of food, who allows his sense of taste to overpower him, loses his independence and easily gets ruined. The greed for food must therefore be destroyed. It is the lesson that I have learn from the fish.

17. There was a dancing girl named Pingala in the town of Videha. She was tired of looking for customers one night. She became hopeless. Then she was contented with what she had, and then had sound sleep. I have learnt from that fallen woman the lesson that the abandonment of hope leads to contentment.
18. A raven picked up a piece of flesh. It was pursued and beaten by other birds. It dropped the piece of flesh and attained peace and rest. From this I have learnt the lesson that a man in the world undergoes all sorts of troubles and miseries when he runs after sensual pleasures, and that he becomes as happy as the bird when he abandons the sensual pleasures.
19. The child who sucks milk is free from all cares, worries and anxieties, and is always cheerful. I have learnt the virtue of cheerfulness from the child.
20. The parents of a maiden had gone in search of a proper bridegroom for her. The girl was alone in the house. During the absence of the parents, a party of people came to the house to see her on a similar object in reference to an offer of marriage. She received the party herself. She went inside to husk the paddy. While she was husking, the glass bangles on both hands made tremendous jingling noise. The wise girl reflected thus: "The party will detect, by the noise of the bangles, that I am husking the paddy myself, and that my family is too poor to engage others to get the work done. Let me break all my bangles except two on each hand". Accordingly, she broke all the bangles except two on each hand. Even these two bangles created much noise. She broke one more bangle of each hand. There was no further noise though she continued husking. I have learnt from the girl's experience the following: Living among many would create discord, disturbance, dispute and quarrel. Even among two, there might be unnecessary words or strife. The ascetic or the Sannyasin should remain alone in solitude.
21. A serpent does not build its hole. It dwells in the holes dug out by others. Even so, an ascetic or a Sannyasin should not build a home for himself. He should live in the caves and temples built by others. This is the lesson that I have learnt from the snake.
22. The mind of an arrow maker was once wholly engrossed in sharpening and straightening an arrow. While he was thus engaged, a king passed before his shop with his whole retinue.

After some time, a man came to the artisan and asked him whether the king passed by his shop. The artisan replied that he did not notice anything. The fact is that the artisan's mind was solely absorbed in his work and he did not know what was passing before his shop. I have learnt from the artisan the quality of intense concentration of mind.

23. The Spider pours out of its mouth long threads and weaves them into cobwebs. It gets itself entangled in the net of its own making. Even so, man makes a net of his own ideas and gets entangled in it. The wise man should therefore abandon all worldly thoughts and think of Brahman only. This is the lesson I have learnt from the spider.
24. The Bhrungi or the Beetle catches hold of a worm, puts it in its nest, and gives it a sting, the poor worm, always fearing the return of the beetle and sting, and thinking constantly of the beetle, becomes a beetle itself. Whatever form a man constantly thinks of, he attains in course of time that form. As a man thinks, so he becomes (As is the mind, so is the marriage). I have learnt from the beetle and the worm to turn myself into Atman by contemplating constantly on It and thus to give up all attachment to the body and attain Moksha or liberation.

Some texts about Dattatreya Guru

The Uddhava Gita, a sequel to the Bhagavad Gita, is a discourse by Lord Krishna to his devotee Uddhava just before Krishna's departure from the world, covering the final teachings and wisdom imparted by Krishna. It's a dialogue between Krishna and Uddhava, occurring shortly before Krishna's departure from the material world.

The teachings of Dattatreya are also found in the Uddhava Gita, a part of the Shrimad Bhagavatam (11.6.40). His teachings emphasize detachment from material desires and ego, promoting the path of self-realization and the realization of the divine presence within oneself and all beings. He is revered as a supreme guru and avatara, a divine being who has attained the highest stage of yogis, and is considered the embodiment of knowledge, compassion, and truth. Dattatreya is believed to have descended to earth to establish universal truth, cosmic order, and dharma, and is ordained with the three energies of the divine powers. Dattatreya is considered immortal, capable of taking any form, and is seen as a god rather than a human being who has become immortal.

The Uddhava Gita explores topics discussed in the Bhagavad Gita in greater depth, offering philosophy, poetry, practical guidance, and hope for a more complete consciousness. It's found in the 11th canto of the Shrimad Bhagavatam, specifically from verse 40 of section 6 through the end of section 29.
The Uddhava Gita aims to guide devotees towards renunciation of worldly attachments and complete dedication to God. It is also known as Hamsa Gita. It consists of 23 chapters. The text delves into spiritual wisdom, Bhakti (devotion) and Saranagati (surrender), with the goal of achieving liberation. It is considered a valuable resource for understanding Krishna's teachings and achieving spiritual enlightenment.

The Avadhoota Gita is a text attributed to the Lord Dattatreya, considered a profound treatise on Advaita Vedanta, the philosophy of non-duality (Advaita), expressing the experience of Brahman, the ultimate reality.

The Avadhuta Gita, meaning "Song of the Free Soul", is a small text of 8 chapters written in Sanskrit verses. It is attributed to the Lord Dattatreya, who is said to have spontaneously sung it after achieving a state of bliss and oneness with Reality.

The text is a powerful expression of Advaita Vedanta, emphasising the non-dual nature of reality and the ultimate unity of the self (Atman) with Brahmam.

Avadhoota – The term refers to a realised soul who has transcended worldly attachments and lives beyond the limitations of the body and mind.

Brahmam – The ultimate reality, the source and ground of all existence.

Atman – The individual self, ultimately identical with Brahman.

The Avadhuta Gita does not engage in philosophical arguments to prove its points, but rather presents direct statements and insights into the nature of reality, leaving the reader to experience the truth for themselves.

Advaita Vedantins have highly valued the Avadhoota Gita and Swami Vivekananda, a prominent Advaitin, often quoted from it.

Dattatreya Upanishad – This text, part of the Atharva Veda, speaks of Dattatreya taking various forms[3] to help his followers attain enlightenment. The Dattatreya Upanishad declares that Lord Dattatreya is the Supreme Reality and the cause of everything that is created.

The text is a Tantra and Vaishnava work, likely one of the relatively recent, 14th or 15th century C.E. composition compared to other Upanishads. The text presents a Vaishnava mantra that is the most popular mantra in Dattatreya tradition, as well as a series of tantric mantras for the worship of Lord Dattatreya, a form of Vishnu. The text asserts that the worship of Vishnu, Narayana and Dattatreya leads one to the nature of Truth-Bliss-Knowledge.

Dattatreya Samhita – The Dattatreya Samhita is a text that explores yoga, particularly focusing on the path to self-realisation and spiritual enlightenment.

The text introduces mantra yoga (repeating mantras), Laya yoga (dissolving the mind) and hatha yoga, all leading to samadhi (a state of deep meditation).

It describes an eightfold yoga, similar to Patanjali's eight limbs and also mentions ten exercises (called as mudras). The Samhita mentions various asanas (postures) and mudras, including Shavasana (corpse pose) and *Viparītakaraṇī* (inverted posture).

---

[3] The different forms of Dattareya are discussed in the next chapter.

It also describes pranayama (breath control) practices like kumbhaka (breath retention) and alternate nostril breathing. The Samhita is attributed to Dattatreya. Dattatreya's philosophy combines Vedantic and Yogic teachings, emphasizing self-realization and spiritual enlightenment.

Let us all understand and surrender to Sri Dattatreya, described in the Puranas.

*****

Different Forms of *Sri Dattatreya*

In general, the form of *Sri Dattatreya* is seen with three heads, six hands, in a naked posture, with four dogs and one cow behind.

Symbolism – Four Dogs – The four dogs that always accompany Dattatreya are seen as embodiments of the four Vedas, representing the ultimate truth. They follow the Lord as "hounds of heaven, watchdogs of the ultimate Truth". They help the Lord in 'hunting' and finding pure souls, wherever they may be born. Behind the Lord Dattatreya is the cow named Kamadhenu – Cow – Mother Earth, in the form of a cow, is said to have sought Dattatreya's protection, highlighting his power and compassion.

In Hindu spirituality, in general, Dattatreya is revered as an Avadhoota sanyasi and while he is known to have many incarnations, the 16 most significant are considered the "*Shodasha Avatars*". These include Yogiraj, Atrivarada, Dattatreya, and others, each embodying a unique facet of divinity.

Householder Form – Dattatreya is known for his avadhoota ascetic lifestyle and is considered an Avadhoota (Jivanmukta), a liberated soul who transcends the limitations of the material world. However, Dattatreya is also said to have a householder form, with Anagha Devi as his consort.

Anagha Devi – the Female form of Lord Dattatreya is referred to as Anagha Devi. It has to be understood as; God cannot be classified as male and female. He is also she and she is also he. Whatever the appearances are, the original form of Shakti/ energy is beyond the gender differentiation, we might not even find out in which aspects or in what form the

Shakti is present among us. One of such examples is the story of Anagha Devi, who is the manifestation of Anagha Deva.

Born out of the yogic energy of Lord Dattatreya, Anagha Devi is portrayed as a very beautiful woman with a bright face. There are many incarnations of Lord Dattatreya and one of them is Anagha Devi (a householder form). Anagha Devi rests in a lotus position wearing an anklet embroidered with bells. She carries a lotus in one hand and shows the sign of protection on the other hand. Depicting the love towards Lord Dattatreya, she is in the state of yoga with her eyes half-closed.

Once when Lord Dattatreya disappeared in a pond at the age of 5, many sages/ his followers waited for his return, thus staying by the pond's bank. Returning from the state of Samadhi after 100 years, Lord Dattatreya decided to test his followers who waited for his return. Thus, from his yogic energy came out his beautiful female avatar.

Female Datta then presented herself drinking wine, overflown in her dancing movement. Unknown to Devi's youthful origin, some called her Madhumati (seeing her drinking wine), some called her Nadi (seeing her dance like a river), still some realized her true form (as Lord Dattatreya's creation) and worshipped her as female Dattatreya.

After everyone's opinion about the lady, Lord Dattatreya came out of the pond and named his yogic energy as *Anagha*[4] (one who is sinless). Those who called her Madhumati and Nadi failed to identify the Lord's Leela and saw Anagha Devi as a sinful woman. But those who identified her true form were blessed with prosperity and peace. All their sorrow disappeared. She was not sinful but the one who could take away the sins and sorrow of people's life. Goddess Anagha was also an ascetic and being formed from the divine power of Dattatreya himself, she was considered the wife of Anagha Deva. There is no difference between Anagha Deva/ Anagha Swami and Anagha Devi. Those who see Anagha Devi as Lord Dattatreya and vice versa are said to attain divine benefits.

---

[4] 987th name in Sri Lalita Sahasranamam is *Anaghā* – without any sin or sorrow.

The reason behind this Leela was to make people aware that there is no he and she in God. The Almighty has many forms, or let's say God is both formless and with forms. One who understands this will understand that God is multiform created out of the same energy.

In Sri Lalita Sahasranama also 813th name is *Mūrtā* and 814th name is *Amūrtā* – she is with form and formless (*Rūpa* and *Nirūpa*)

In *Vişŋu Sahasranāma* the 720th name – *Amūrtimān* – he is formless.

Brahadāraŋya Upanishad (II–3–1), *Brahmam* has two forms, *Mūrtā* and *Amūrtā*.

Agha means sorrow, whereas Anagha means sorrowless and sinless. Therefore, the goddess's name itself defines the motive behind her creation. She was created to remove (Agha) the sorrows of her devotees. Lord Dattatreya is often explained as the one who seems to be influenced by Maya, but in actual he is the one who creates Maya.

Anagha Devi is the mother of the world and the embodiment of the knowledge of Lord Dattatreya. Both Anagha Deva and Anagha Devi are said to be free from all kinds of sins and all pillage. Anagha Devi is the power/shakti of Anagha Deva, because of whom, Anagha Deva is able to bestow happiness to his devotees and removes sins from them.

There are very many temples/ shrines for Lord Dattatreya. But it is very rare to see a shrine for Anagha Devi sameta Dattatreya. One such shrine can be seen in the Sri Ganapati Sachidananda Ashram, Baby Nagar, Velachery, Chennai. Incidentally, first Dattatreya temple in Tamilnadu was constructed at Sri Dattagiri, Sendamangalam. There is a temple for Dattar at Prayag, Uttar Pradesh in the name as Guru Murthy.

Parama Pūjya Śrī Ganapati Saccidānanda Swamijī of Śrī Avadhūta Datta Pīţham, Mysore, has established temples for each of 16 avatars of Lord Dattareya. The details of such temples, sixteen avatars with thithis of each incarnation, some description, concerned picture, temple location, etc., are detailed below;

1. First Avatar – Yogiraja – Appeared on Kartika Shuddha Pournami as the manifestation of the combined power of all divinities. Yogiraj is Sarvadevamaya and Sarva Mantra Artha Maya. Datta Yogiraja Temple, Bengaluru, Karnataka.

1. YOGIRAJ

After the creation of this universe the living beings had to suffer from miseries as per their past actions. This made Brahma more anxious and hence he surrendered to Shri Vishnu, the Lord of the universe saying, "*Dattoham Dattoham*" (I give myself).

Lord Vishnu appeared before Brahma and advised him to practice yoga and know the eternal principle whereby he was relieved of the miseries, and had the peace of mind.

Those, who recite "*Dattoham Dattomam*", will also gain the same fruit.

This Avatar propagated yoga, hence it is known as 'Yogeshwar' or 'Yogiraj'. He looked most charming, delicate and snow-white in colour. Like Shri Krishna, he had one head and four hands.

2. Second Avatar – Atri Varada – Kartika Bahula Pradamai – this incarnation indicates Sri Dattatreya as the essence of all Mantras. Atri Varada Dattatreya Temple, Machilipatnam, Andhra Pradesh.

2. ATRI VARADA

When sage Atri lived as a Grihastha, he had many sons. They were learned and erudite, but he longed to have a son, who would be famous in all the three Lokas and would guide the people to attain the highest goal of life. He, therefore, observed severe penance on the Riksha mountain. Due to the luster of his penance, the three Lokas suffered from heat and all the creatures and birds became uneasy. All the Gods, Rishi-Munis approached Brahma, Vishnu and Mahesh. Then Brahma, riding on swan, Vishnu on Garuda and Mahesh on Nandi appeared before Atri and roused him from his meditation. Atri bowed to them and said, "I adored only one God then who are you three?" The three Gods said, "We are the same whom you aimed at. We appear in three forms; but we are one. Maya (illusion) is threefold sattva, raj and tamas. Raj creates, sattva protects and tam destroys. These three powers are prominent. Paramatma possesses all these three powers." Atri was blessed with a son by the three Gods as desired. Hence this Avatar is known as 'Atri Varada'. He had luster like hot gold and a smiling face. This Avatar appeared on Kartik Vadya Pratipada, Rohini Nakshatra, Thursday, first prahar and first muhurta. He had one or three heads and held Brahma's garland and Kamandalu in the lower two hands, God Shiva's drum and Trishool in the middle two hands and Vishnu's conch and chakra in the upper two hands.

3. Third Avatar – Datta Prabhu – Kartika Bahula Dwitiya – Granted himself to sage Atri. Datta Yogiraja Temple, Bengaluru, Karnataka.

Bhagwan Shri Hari appeared before sage Atri as a boy looking bluish as Indranil in colour. His face was pleasant as the Moon, his four hands possessed conch, chakra, gada and Padma.

Vibhuti was applied on his body and he had locks of hair on his head. He appeared saying, *'Dattoham'*. Atri and Anasuya said, "We shall not be content till you take birth from us". Being pleased with their speech, he entered in the heart of Atri as a spark of lightening and afterwards took birth as a son of Anasuya.

4. Fourth Avatara – Kaalaagni Shamana – Margashirsha Shuddha Chaturdashi – Took birth as Atri's son. Avadhoota Datta Peetham's main deity, Mysore, Karnataka.

Amongst the sixteen Avatars of Shri Datta, this fourth Avatar is regarded as most prominent. Due to the hard penance at the Riksha hill, Atri looked very bright and his body became too hot. Bhagwan Shri Hari came to Atri to cool down his heat. Due to this achievement this Avatar is known as 'Kalaagni shaman'. When Atri opened his eyes, he saw before him the most loving Anasuya. The bright luster of his eyes entered in the body of Anasuya Yogi Jana wondered to see this. She entreated the God in humility saying, "I shall not be content until you take birth as a human being from my womb". Subsequently Shri Hari appeared as a newly born baby and lay on her bedstead.

5. Fifth Avatara – Yogi Jana Vallabha – Margashirsha Pournami – indicates the compassion of the Lord towards his devotees. Yogi Raja Vallabha Dattatreya Temple, Proddatur, Andhra Pradesh.

When Sri Dattatreya appeared at Anasuya's ashram, Indra followed by the Devas, Rishi-Munis, Gandharvas, Caranas, Yogis and saints came to see him.

Knowing their eagerness, Shri Datta appeared as a boy and advised them about yoga. He said, "I have no body, no time. I am devoid of birth and death. I take various forms to bless the devotees. Though these acts are transitory this does not affect my Tattva state".

This Avatar is known for the propagation of yoga path and for removing the obstacles coming in the way and blessing the followers of yoga. This Avatar is, therefore, known as "Yogijan Vallabha".

6. Sixth Avatar – Leela Vishwambhara – Pausha Pournami – appeared as a child to protect his devotees. Vishwambara Avadhoota Dattatreya Temple, Akividu, Andhra Pradesh.

The love for children and intense mercifulness of Shri Datta are observed in this Avatar. There was a great famine in the country. Animals could not get food and water. So, they were reduced to boney skeletons. Thieves and dacoits looted the public. Rishi-Munis could not perform their rites and sacrifices were stopped. Rishi-Munis, Brahmins etc. surrendered to Shri Datta, who was lying in the laps of Anasuya and feeding on her breast. Hearing the prayers of the people, Shri Datta appeared as Leela Vishwambhar before them and offered to them food, clothes and provisions and satisfied them all. This was achieved easily and hence he is known as "Leela Vishwambhar". One day Shri Datta addressed the devotees as follows, "This life is like a vast forest. Ahankar is like a big mountain surrounded by big trees, creepers and plants. Kama i.e. cupid is a fierce lion, krodha (anger) is an enraged serpent, vasana (desires) are great lakes. Those, who cannot swim in the water, get drowned". Shri Datta then changed this scene. The devotees, therefore, asked, "Where is the fierce forest?" Shri Datta replied smilingly, "It has immersed whence it was created. It comes into existence due to ignorance and when it is wiped off, it vanishes. Those, who remember me, get rid of the family miseries. All this physical world is destroyable and Atma, which is at the root, is only lasting." The devotees enquired, "How is the Atma?" Shri Datta replied, "I am that Atma. I am known by good action and intense devotion."

7. Seventh Avatar – Siddha Raja – Magha Pournami – Resurrected the system of Yoga as a preparatory step for Gnana. Siddha Raja Dattatreya Temple, Cochin, Kerala

Shri Datta Guru appeared as a boy named Vishwambhar in the Badri forest, where several siddhas were observing penance of different sorts. Some had achieved siddhis and were enjoying many pleasures. Some believed in God, while some did not. Vishwambhar sat in a corner in the assembly of the siddhas. Seeing the lustrous boy, the siddhas asked him;

Q. "Who are you?"
A. "Shri Datta." I am not discernible.
Q. "Which is your abode?"
A. "I have no abode. No one is my master."
Q. "Which is your yoga? What is the mode of your study?"
A. "Mine is Chitra yoga and there is no special mode of my study."
Q. "Which is your mudra?"
A. "Mine is a compassionate Niranjana mudra."
Q. "What do you see in this mudra?"
A. "I see what is beyond meditation. My aim is that principle which is beyond the threefold meditations, meditator and the object of meditation."
Q. "Which is your path?"

A. "My path is that which gives realisation of the Shiva tattva (eternal principle)."

While this dialogue was going on, 11 Rudras, 12 Adityas, 49 Rudra Ganas, Rishis, Munis, Sadhya Deva, Gandharva, Yaksha, Kinnara etc., were passing through the sky. Their motion being hindered, they all came down on the floor of Badrivan. All the siddhas wondered to see this. Each siddha said that because of his penance, their motion was hindered and they came down on the earth.

Shri Datta, in the body-form, said, "Why do you struggle? One, who can remove the hindrance of their motion and allow them to go through the sky, will be the best siddha." All agreed to this and each one came forward and said one after another, "I have removed the obstacle in your movement. You can go to your places." But none of them could move a bit. Then Shri Datta said, "Oh you Rishi-Munis and others, you may please go to your places as the hindrance in your movement has since been removed." Hearing this, all those who had descended, bowed to Shri Datta and flew away in the sky. Seeing this, all the siddhas realised that the boy Yogi was the Paramatma. They, therefore, gave up their vanity and surrendered to him.

The boy Yogi, Shri Datta, said, "I am 'Siddharaj', 'Yogiraj'. I am called 'Hari' being Kalagni shaman and remover of miseries. While thinking about Atma and in order to attain me, one should study mantras. I am Mantraraj, undestroyable and Parabrahma. All the universe is under my control; but I am controlled by mantras. All mantras, studied as per due procedure, give siddhi (power of doing certain things) to Sadhak." Saying this, he further told them some mantras and their procedure. This is known as 'Siddha Rajagam'. Shri Datta told this again, about 500 years ago, to his great favourite devotee Dasopant of Ambejogai (Maharashtra), who has preserved it in a written script. The publication of 'Siddha Rajagam' will be truly most valuable and appreciable.

8.GNAANA SAGARA

8. Eighth Avatara – Gnana Sagara – Phalguna Shuddha Dashami – indicated the

necessity of Gnana for liberation. Gnaana Saagara Dattatreya Temple, Anantapur, Andhra Pradesh.

Bhagwan Shri Dattatreya once contemplated, "These persons have achieved yoga siddhis etc. Still, until kama, krodha, lobha etc. are not conquered by them, they would not have real peace of mind and they will have no pleasure. Kama i.e. desire, is at the root of all the miseries and everyone is struggling in his life to get one's desires fulfilled. Krodha i.e. anger, follows desires. All the world is engrossed in this struggle and is suffering from threefold miseries viz. physical, metaphysical and mental. Therefore, all the people should be above the bondage of kama, krodha, lobha, etc., then they will gain knowledge and attain my place." Hence, Shri Datta appeared in the form of a Kumar known as "Gnana Sagar".

The siddhas tried to bring this Kumar on the ground; but they could not do so. They, therefore, realised that he was Paramatma and surrendered to him and began to praise him.

Shri Datta then said, "Kama begets anger, anger begets delusion of intellect and untoward actions take place. Those, who go after siddhis, do not get my place and consequently they do not get pleasure.

Therefore, you should adore me, recite mantras and know the eternal principle and lead a moral life. You cannot gain me by intellect or logic, without longing for the fruit. So, one should win over kama, krodha etc. and continue my devotion. The siddhas thereafter followed the path, shown by Shri Datta and attained the bliss. This Avatar took place in Badrivan for the well-being of the siddhas, who were staying there.

9. Ninth Avatara – Vishwambhar Avadhoota – Chaitra Pournami –

Established Bhakti Yoga. Vishwambara Avadhoota Dattatreya Temple, Akividu, Andhra Pradesh.

With a view to test the siddhas and see how far they have progressed, Shri Datta assumed the dirty form of a mleccha. His face was robust. He had black string round his neck, a zigzag stick in his hand and a black dog followed him. He saw that some siddhas were meditating, while some were enjoying the jokes and some others suffering from miseries. The siddhas asked him questions as before and he replied in the same style.

Then realising him to be Shri Datta, they surrendered to him and began to praise him. Shri Datta then appeared before them in his usual lovely form and advised them to give up doubts and concentrate their minds on him.

10. Tenth Avatara – Maya Mukta Avadhoota – Jyeshtha Shuddha Trayodashi – Grants worldly desires of his devotees. Maaya Mukta Avadhoota Dattatreya Temple, Achcharapakam, Tamil Nadu

Shri Datta appeared in the form of a mendicant (*bairagi*) at the house of one pious devotee, named Sheel. He was performing the anniversary rites and brahmins were invited. He looked handsome and had golden luster. He had a pot in one hand for the alms and a stick in the right hand. There was a wreath of rudrakshas round his neck. The brahmins, who were invited, got enraged to see the bairagi. They asked him, "Who are you?"

The bairagi said, "I am undiscernible, all-pervading Avadhoot." Hearing this, Sheel knew that he was Siddhraj Dynan Sagar of former times. To remove his doubt, he asked, "What is your abode (Ashraya) and who is your master?" The reply was, "I have no abode and no master. I am the master of all the three Lokas." Realising him to be his Sadguru, he prostrated before him, seated him with due regard, duly worshipped him and offered him good delicious food. Seeing this, the brahmins scolded Sheel, saying that he acted un piously.

The mendicant then asked the brahmins, "What is Brahmanam?" The brahmins said, "Om is Parabrahma and it has assumed the form of Vedas. You are unpious and irreligious and so you are not eligible even to hear Vedas." The mendicant said, "I am above Maya and hence not bound by rules and regulations. Vedas and their acts are of three qualities and this world is also three-fold and it is with me in the form of a black dog. This dog is well-versed in Vedas and shastras. He will satisfy you." Saying so, he asked the dog to say Vedas. Like a learned pandit the dog began to chant the Vedas. The brahmins were simply stunned to see this miracle.

Shri Avadhoot called the forefathers of Sheel and in the presence of all assimilated them in himself. The vanity of the brahmins was wiped off and they surrendered to Shri Datta, who advised them to have devotion for him. This pleased them all. They prayed to him to bestow on them the lasting well-being of their families.

11. Eleventh Avatar – Maya Yukta Avadhoota – Vaishakha Shuddha Chaturdashi – Destroys Kama in his devotees.

This Avatar appeared in a young meditating pose, having a beautiful young woman on his left lap. Knowing them as Lakshmi-Narayan, all narrated their family short comings; but none showed a liking for the spiritual matters. Shri Datta began to sing and dance with the young woman. People thought that Shri Datta was playing with Maya and they did not leave him. Shri Datta then brought forward flesh, wine and similar unpious articles and said, "I am enjoying all these things, so I have no power and ability to fulfil your desires." Hearing this, many persons forsook him and only few remained there. Shri Datta then told them, "Faith, devotion, meditation, practising rules of Sama, dana and by conquering the desires the human beings can get rid of the family bondages."

Then Mayayukta Avadhoot roamed in the region from the south of Narmada to the Mahur hills. The Devas, harassed by Jambasur, Kartavirya – Sahasrarjun and Parashuram met Shri Datta in this region. Shri Datta advised, "Tripura Rahasya" to Parashuram in order to get rid of the effects of his sins of wars against the kshatriyas and to attain the peace of mind.

12. Twelfth Avatar – Adi Guru – Aashaadha Pournami – Grants Brahma Gnana to Uttamadhikaris. Aadi Guru Dattatreya Temple, Chennai, Tamilnadu.

Alarka prayed Dattatreya. Shri Datta advised Alark, the son of Madalsa. While ruling as a king, Alark was engrossed in the worldly pleasures. Dnyani Subahu, his elder brother, thought that Alark was wasting away his life as dogs and cats do in enjoyment of passions. He intended to awaken him spiritually. He, therefore, came to his city and asked for his share in the kingdom. When it was refused, he sought the help of Kashi Raja and attacked and besieged his city. Consequently, the provisions coming in the city were stopped. Due to this, the subjects could not get food grains and they began to suffer from hunger. Alark was dejected to see this. His mother, Madalsa, had told him to see her letter of advice, placed in the box in times of calamity. He left the city, entered a forest and next morning opened the box and saw his dear mother's letter. It was said in it that in times of adversity, one should forsake all and have the company of a saint and think of salvation. He should go to Shri Datta at Mahurgad for spiritual guidance.

Alark went to Mahur, surrendered to Shri Datta and narrated his misery. Shri Datta placed his palm on his head and asked, "Where is your misery? Just think who you are." Only due to this one question,

Alark began to think of himself. His ignorance was wiped off and his ego and greed also vanished. The feeling of enmity was extinct.

13. Thirteenth Avathara – Sri Shiva Roopa Dattatreya – Shravana Pournami – Grants Sayujya to Madhyamadhikaris. Samskaara Heena Shivaroopa Dattatreya Temple, Jayalakshmipuram (Bommeparti), Andhra Pradesh.

Pingalnag, a pious brahmin knowing Veda shastra lived at Mahur. He saw a lustrous youth under a black awala tree. The youth had a naked young woman. He knew Vedas. Pingalnag asked him, "Who are you? You do not look to be pious; but you say Vedas. You have not the 'Dand' of a Brahmacharini Agnihotri of a grihastha. Your age is not due for proceeding a sannyasin. Then which is your ashram?" The youth said, "All the universe is Atma roop. Mine is the fifth ashram, who sees Atma everywhere."

Pingalnag recognised him as Shri Dattatreya, the son of Anasuya and so bowed to him humbly and prayed to bless him and give proper advice.

14. Fourteenth Avatar – Sri Deva Deva – Bhadrapada Shuddha Chaturdashi – grants Atmapada to his devotees. Deva Deva Dattatreya Temple, Nuzvid, Andhra Pradesh.

Shri Datta roamed from the south of Narmada to Mahur in the forest. He bathed in rivers, lakes, at holy places and gave darshan to Rushi-Munis. This region was full of black awala trees and so it was called 'Krishna Malaki Tirth'.

The Devas, Brahma, Shatanand, son of sage Goutam had come and seen Shri Datta here.

Note; Among the Ekadasha Rudras, the 9th Rudra is called as Deva Devar (God of all gods).

15. Fifteenth Avathara – Sri Digambara – Aswayuja Pournami – to establish Vairagya. Digambara Datta Temple, Rishikesh, Uttarakhand.

In this Avatar Shri Datta blessed Yadu of Somvansh and Prahlad, son of Kayadhu. When Yadu Raja was wandering in the forest in the Kaveri region, he saw a Digambar Avadhoot. He prostrated before him and said, "You are young, lustrous and healthy and then why do you stay in such a desolate forest and yet you are joyful and carefree."

Digambar Avadhoot said, "I have acquired 24 Gurus from nature and learnt lessons of different types from them. Thus, I have acquired Vivek, vairagya, peace of mind and contentment.

16. Sixteenth Avathara – Sri Krishna Shyama Kamalanayana – Kartika Shuddha Dwadashi – complete with sixteen Kalas, is the complete manifestation of the Lord. Shyaamakamala Lochana Dattatreya Temple, Vijayawada, Andhra Pradesh.

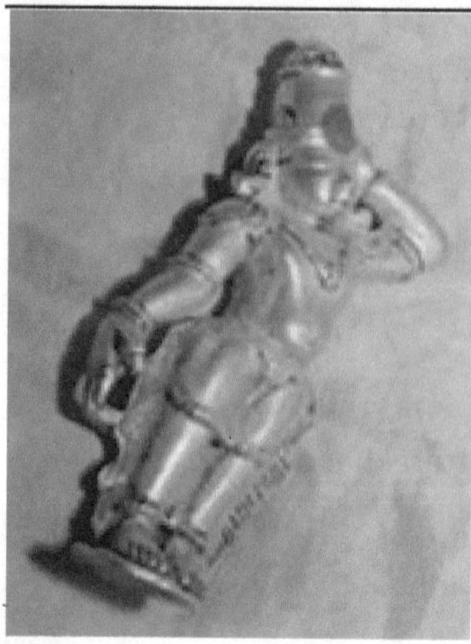

Shri Datta had different Avatars as Yogiraj, Atri Varad etc. and advised his devotees with Dhyan, bhakti, vairagya, eight-fold yoga sadhana etc.

Bhagwan Shri Datta was lying on the bed of Dhyan and was engrossed in yoga. At that time, some devotees and disciples came to see him. Shri Datta appeared pleasant and in the form of Sat Chit (lasting and lustrous).

Shri Datta said, "Having studied all the shastras, I tell you the real essence. Practising it you will soon get salvation. Vedic dharma is ever lasting. Veda is at its root; hence dharma has prominence and lasting status. I am 'Datta' not only for Atri, but I give myself to all those who have unprejudiced devotion for me. I give sayujyata (i.e. merging with myself) to such devotees."

In addition to the above list, Dattatreya is believed to have taken various forms to guide humanity, including;

- Shripada Vallabhar – Considered as the first incarnation of Dattatreya in the current cycle of time viz. Kali Yug.
- Narasimha Saraswati – Another important incarnation, known for his teachings and spiritual practices.
- Swami Samarth – Another important incarnation.
- Gagangiri Maharaj
- Manik Prabhu
- Gajanan Maharaj
- Sai Baba of Shirdi
- Shreedhar Swami

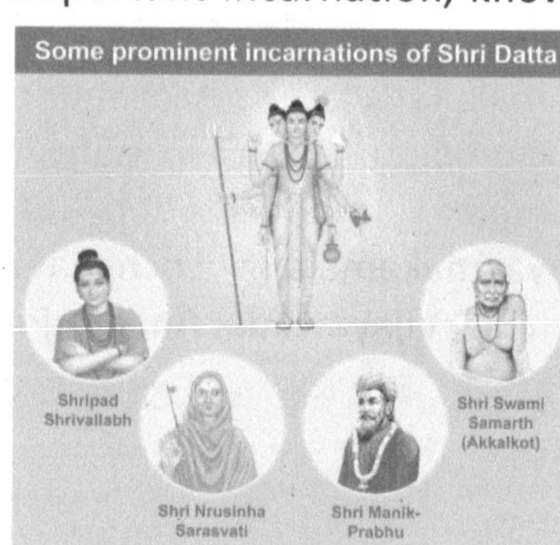

Let us all understand the truth that no matter how many forms and incarnations he takes, he is all one and the same Dattatreya and worship him and become enlightened.

Though we celebrate Datta Jayanti only once a year, a sincere Upasaka should worship Dattatreya on the sixteen auspicious Tithis, detailed in the previous chapter to achieve Siddhi of Sri Dattatreya Anushtup Maha mantra.

*****

Śrī Dattātreya Yantra

It is usual to worship Gods through *mantras, tantras* and *yantras*. Worshipping through *mantras* is called *Māntrīka* method. Worshipping through *tantras* is called *Tāntrīka* method. Worshipping through *yantras* is called *Vaidhīka* method. Whichever be the method *mantras* are definitely used to worship. But which is predominant is to be considered.

Mantras, the sound form of deities, are integral to *Sādhanas* (worship). *Mantra* pertaining to each God/ Goddess will have different number of letters called *chandas*. Similarly, each God/ Goddess will have various *mantras* – probably each one for a particular purpose/ satiating a desire.

Tantras (Looms or Weavings) refer to numerous and varied scriptures pertaining to any of several esoteric traditions rooted in philosophy of the religion. The religious culture of the *Tantras* is essentially *Tāntric* material can be shown to have been derived from earlier *Vedic* sources. And although *Tantras* of different religions have many similarities from the outside, internally they do have some clear distinctions.

Yantras are some mathematical drawings/ patterns used for worship. There are mathematical construction methods explaining the drawing of *yantras*. *Yantras* mean originally the mechanical, mnemonic and musical contraption in the macrocosm. It is a graphic symbol of the contemplative meditation in the tradition, which was intended to be unified with the Gods/ goddesses. *Yantras* area also called as *cakras*. In a human body itself we have seven cakras thought to be an energy point or node in the subtle body viz., *Mūlādhārā, Swādhişţānā, Maṇipūrakā, Anāhatā, Viśuddha, Agjnā* and *Sahasrārā*.

Sri Lalita Sahasranama, names 204, 205 and 206, *Sarva Mantra Svarūpiŋī, Sarva Yantrātmikā* and *Sarva Tantrarūpā*. That is, Sri Lalita herself is in the form of all the *Mantras, Yantras* and *Tantras*.

Usually when consecrating an idol of a deity, it is customary to place the *yantras* of the respective deity beneath the respective idol, duly drawn on copper or five-metals or silver or gold, etc. Properly drawn *yantras* emit micro-vibrations. Those vibrations are not feelable by human beings. However, they have a huge impact on our body, mainly positive impact. It is customary to worship the concerned deity alongwith the respective *chakras/ yantras*.

Yantras are great cosmic conductors of energy, an antenna of Nature, a powerful tool for harmony, prosperity, success, good health, yoga and meditation. *Yantras* are usually made out of copper and consist of a series of geometric patterns. The eyes and mind concentrate at the center of the yantra to achieve higher levels of consciousness.

Dattatreya Yantra

Lord Dattatreya is unique because he is believed to be the combined form of Brahma, Vishnu, and Shiva, representing the perfect harmony of creation, preservation, and destruction. This makes him an essential figure in the understanding of the balance of the universe.

The Dattatreya Yantra is a sacred, symbol representing the trinity of Shiva, Vishnu and Brahma, embodied in Lord Dattatreya and is used in Pooja ceremonies for blessings, protection and spiritual development.

The Dattatreya Yantra is a powerful spiritual instrument that symbolizes the collective divine energies of the Trimurti (Brahma, Vishnu, and Shiva). The Dattatreya yantra is a highly significant and powerful tool for self-transformation and spiritual growth. This yantra depicts the energy of the divine being Dattatreya, who is known as the Avatar of the Supreme Self. By meditating on this yantra, we can connect with the powerful energy of Dattatreya and receive his blessings.

The Dattatreya Yantra composed of nine triangles and hence, it is known as the *Navayoni* Chakra. These nine triangles are of various sizes and intersect with one another. In the middle is the power point (*Bindu*), visualizing the highest, the invisible, elusive center from which the entire figure and the cosmos expand.

This yantra can help us to overcome our ego, develop our spiritual practice, and become more self-aware. It is also said to help attract abundance and prosperity. By meditating on this yantra, we can receive the grace and guidance of Dattatreya, and attain a higher level of consciousness.

This Yantra is used for the worship of Lord Jupiter for prosperity, power, rank, authority, abundance, wealth, business. The yantra can be placed near the entrance of the home/ office/ shop or in the living room, reception, study room or office cabin. The ideal place is to hang it on the wall of puja room, living room or office facing North or East direction. It is used in Pooja ceremonies and is believed to aid in overcoming obstacles, achieving success, and maintaining mental peace and stability. Other benefits of worshipping Dattatreya Yantra;

- It removes the effects of Pitru (ancestors) Dosha.
- It aids those who are under the influence of evil forces.
- It protects you from the bad intentions of others.
- It removes unknown hindrances to success in all aspects of their lives.
- Dattatreya yantra helps to increase material wealth and success.
- It helps to improve spiritual enlightenment and guidance.
- It benefits to protect against negative influences and energies.
- Dattatreya yantra also improves concentration and focus.
- It helps to bring about overall good fortune.

Devotees who worship and meditate with this Yantra are believed to receive divine blessings, leading to a fulfilling and spiritually enriched life.

It is often made of copper or silver or gold or five-metals, which is considered sacred and auspicious in Hindu traditions.

*****

Śrī Dattātreya Mantras

श्री दत्तात्रेय मन्त्रा:

Lord Dattatreya, who is in the form of the trinity gods, is considered the original earliest (Aadi) guru of the Avadhoota Sanyasa lineage. His mantras are capable of bestowing all the benefits to everyone.

Śrī Dattātreya Mantrāḥ – श्री दत्तात्रेय मन्त्रा:

1. *Śrī Dattātreya Ṣaḍākṣarī Mantraḥ* (6 lettered mantra) – श्री दत्तात्रेय षडाक्षरी मन्त्र:

Oṃ Śrīṃ Hrīṃ Klīṃ Glauṃ Drāṃ – ओं श्रीं ह्रीं क्लीं ग्लौं द्रां

2. *Śrī Dattātreya Aṣṭākṣarī Mantraḥ* (8 lettered mantra) – श्री दत्तात्रेय अष्टाक्षरी मन्त्र:

Oṃ Drāṃ Dattātreyāya Namaḥ – ओं द्रां दत्तात्रेयाय नम:

3. *Śrī Dattātreya Dvādaśākṣarī Mantraḥ* (12 lettered mantra) – श्री दत्तात्रेय द्वादशाक्षरी मन्त्र:

Oṃ Āṃ Hrīṃ Kroṃ Ehyehi Dattātreyāya Namaḥ –
ओं आं ह्रीं क्रों एह्येहि दत्तात्रेयाय नम:

4. *Śrī Dattātreya Ṣhoḍaśākṣarī Mantraḥ* (16 lettered mantra) – श्री दत्तात्रेय षोडशाक्षरी मन्त्र:

Oṃ Aiṃ Kroṃ Klīṃ Klūṃ Hrāṃ Hrīṃ Hrūṃ Sauḥ Dattātreyāya Svāhā – ओं ऐं क्रों क्लीं क्लूं ह्रां ह्रीं ह्रूं सौ: दत्तात्रेयाय स्वाहा

5. *Śrī Dattātreya Gāyatri Mantraḥ* – *Oṃ Śrī Dattātreyāya Vidmahe, Digambarāya Dīmahi Tanno Datta Pracodayāt.*

6. *Śrī Dattātreya Mālā Mantraḥ* – श्री दत्तात्रेय माला मन्त्र:

Note; This *Mālā Mantram* is part of *Dattātreya Upanishad.*

Śrī Gaṇeśāya Namaḥ ।

Pārvatyuvāca |

Mālāmantraṃ Mama Brūhi Priyāyasmādahaṃ Tava |

Īśvara Uvāca –

Śṛṇu Devi Pravakṣyāmi Mālāmantramanuttamam ||

Oṃ Namo Bhagavate Dattātreyāya, Smaraṇamātrasantuṣṭāya,
Mahābhayanivāraṇāya Mahājñānapradāya, Cidānandātmane,
Bālonmattapiśācaveṣāya, Mahāyogine, Avadhūtāya, Anaghāya,
Anasūyānandavardhanāya Atriputrāya, Sarvakāmaphalapradāya,
Oṃ Bhavabandhavimocanāya, Āṃ Asādhyasādhanāya,
Hrīṃ Sarvavibhūtidāya, Krauṃ Asādhyākarṣaṇāya,
Aiṃ Vākpradāya, Klīṃ Jagatrayavaśīkaraṇāya,
Sauḥ Sarvamanaḥkṣobhaṇāya, Śrīṃ Mahāsampatpradāya,
Glauṃ Bhūmaṃḍalādhipatyapradāya, Drāṃ Ciraṃjīvine,
Vaṣaṭvaśīkuru Vaśīkuru, Vauṣaṭ Ākarṣaya Karayi,
Huṃ Vidveṣaya Viviana, Phaṭ Uccāṭaya Cutaia,
Ṭhaḥ Than Staṃbhaya Shambhala, Kheṃ Khem Māraya Maraya,
Namaḥ Sampannaya Samp Annaya, Svāhā Poṣaya Posay,
Paramantraparayantraparatantrāṇi Chiṃdhi Chimdi,
Grahānnivāraya Nivāraya, Vyādhīn Vināśaya Vinaya,
Duḥkhaṃ Hara Vinaya, Dāridryaṃ Vidrāvaya Vidyalaya,
Dehaṃ Poṣaya Daham, Cittaṃ Toṣaya Tusayan,
Sarvamantrasvarūpāya, Sarvayantrasvarūpāya,
Sarvatantrasvarūpāya, Sarvapallavasvarūpāya,
Oṃ Namo Mahāsiddhāya Svāhā |

Iti Dattātreyopaniśadī Śrī Datta Mālā Mantraḥ Sampūrṇaḥ |

श्री दत्त माला मन्त्रः ।

श्री गणेशाय नमः ।

पार्वत्युवाच -

मालामन्त्रं मम ब्रूहि प्रियायस्मादहं तव ।

ईश्वर उवाच -

शृणु देवि प्रवक्ष्यामि मालामन्त्रमनुत्तमम् ॥

ॐ नमो भगवते दत्तात्रेयाय, स्मरणमात्रसन्तुष्टाय, महाभयनिवारणाय महाज्ञानप्रदाय,
चिदानन्दात्मने, बालोन्मत्तपिशाचवेषाय, महायोगिने, अवधूताय, अनघाय,
अनसूयानन्दवर्धनाय अत्रिपुत्राय, सर्वकामफलप्रदाय,
ॐ भवबन्धविमोचनाय, आं असाध्यसाधनाय,
ह्रीं सर्वविभूतिदाय, क्रौं असाध्याकर्षणाय, ऐं वाक्प्रदाय, क्लीं जगत्रयवशीकरणाय,
सौः सर्वमनःक्षोभणाय, श्रीं महासम्पत्प्रदाय, ग्लौं भूमंडलाधिपत्यप्रदाय,
द्रां चिरंजीविने, वषट्वशीकुरु वशीकुरु, वौषट् आकर्षय आकर्षय,
हुं विद्वेषय विद्वेषय, फट् उच्चाटय उच्चाटय, ठः ठः स्तंभय स्तंभय,
खें खें मारय मारय, नमः सम्पन्नय सम्पन्नय, स्वाहा पोषय पोषय,
परमन्त्रपरयन्त्रपरतन्त्राणि छिंधि छिंधि, ग्रहान्निवारय निवारय,
व्याधीन् विनाशय विनाशय, दुःखं हर हर, दारिद्र्यं विद्रावय विद्रावय,
देहं पोषय पोषय, चित्तं तोषय तोषय, सर्वमन्त्रस्वरूपाय, सर्वयन्त्रस्वरूपाय,
सर्वतन्त्रस्वरूपाय, सर्वपल्लवस्वरूपाय, ॐ नमो महासिद्धाय स्वाहा ।

इति दत्तात्रेयोपनिशदी श्रीदत्त माला मन्त्रः सम्पूर्णः ।

A Datta Yogi in Andhra Desha said affirmatively a tip thus – "If one recites the great Dattatreya Mantras, having duly received it from Sadguru, sixteen thousand times on each of these sixteen Tithis, he will surely see Dattatreya". The Datta Anushtup Mantra itself is a concise summary of the essence of these sixteen Avataras and holds the key to the secret of Dattatreya Tattva. Uttamadhikaris should learn the significance of the Mantra and its Dharana in the sixteen Chakras in the body to achieve oneness with Vishwa Guru. This mantra is the most ancient and the king among the other 32 mantras of Sri Dattatreya.

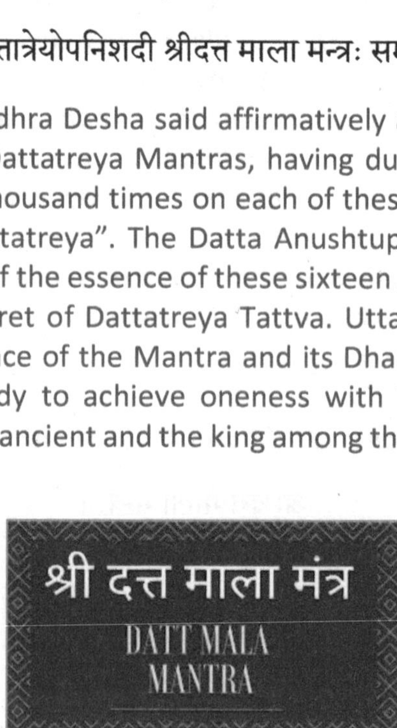

*****

Ādi Guru Śiva Datta Nāma Puja

Dhyānam

Dattātrēya Harē Krişṇa Uṉmattāṉanta Dāyaka ।
Digampara Muṉē Pāla Piśāca Ñāṉa Sāgara ॥

Oṃ Mālā Kamaṇḍaluradhaḥ Karapadmayugme
Madhyasthapāṇiyugale Ḍamarutriśūle ।
Yannyasta Ūrdhvakarayoḥ Śubhaśaṅkhacakre
Vande Tamatrivaradaṃ Bhujaṣaṭka Yuktam ॥

Śrī Dattātrēya Gurum Dyāyāmi | Āvāhayāmi |
Āsaṉam Samarpayāmi ।
Pādayōḥ Pādyam Samarpayāmi ।
Hastayōḥ Argyam Samarpayāmi ।

Ācamaṉīyam Samarpayāmi । *Madhuparkam Samarpayāmi* ।
Śuddhōtaka Sṉāṉam Samarpayāmi ।
Sṉāṉantaram Ācamaṉīyam Samarpayāmi ।

Vastram Samarpayāmi ।
Yañjōpavīta, Āparaṇāṉiñca Samarpayāmi ।
Divya Parimaḷa Gantāṉ Dārayāmi ।
Gantasya Upari Haridrā Kuṅkumam Samarpayāmi ।
Akṣatāṉ Samarpayāmi । *Puṣpamālāṉ Samarpayāmi* ।
Puṣpaiḥ Sampūjayāmi ।

Śrī Dattātrēya Guru Ṣōṭaśa Nāmāvaḷiḥ

1. *Oṃ Drām Oṃ Tattātrēya Namaḥ* ।
2. *Oṃ Drām Oṃ Aṉasūyāsutāya Namaḥ* ।
3. *Oṃ Drām Oṃ Tattāya Namaḥ* ।
4. *Oṃ Drām Oṃ Atriputrāya Namaḥ* ।
5. *Oṃ Drām Oṃ Mahāmuṉayē Namaḥ* ।
6. *Oṃ Drām Oṃ Yōkīntrāya Namaḥ* ।
7. *Oṃ Drām Oṃ Puṇya Puruṣāya Namaḥ* ।
8. *Oṃ Drām Oṃ Tēvēśāya Namaḥ* ।

9. *Oṃ Drām Oṃ Jakatīśvarāya Namaḥ* I
10. *Oṃ Drām Oṃ Paramātmaṉē Namaḥ* I
11. *Oṃ Drām Oṃ Paraprahmaṇē Namaḥ* I
12. *Oṃ Drām Oṃ Satāṉantāya Namaḥ* I
13. *Oṃ Drām Oṃ Jakatkuravē Namaḥ* I
14. *Oṃ Drām Oṃ Nityatruptāya Namaḥ* I
15. *Oṃ Drām Oṃ Nirākārāya Namaḥ* I
16. *Oṃ Drām Oṃ Nirvikārāya Namaḥ* I

In brief only 16 names are given above. Those who want to perform arcana with 108 or 1008 names, they are given in separate chapters.

Śrī Dattātrēya Guravē Namaḥ Nāṉāvita Parimaḷa Patra Puṣpāṇi Samarpayāmi I

Śrī Tattātrēyakuru Mūla Mantram –
Oṃ Ām Hrīm Krōm Ēhi Dattātrēya Svāhā I I (4 Times)

Śrī Dattātrēya Guravē Namaḥ Dhūpamāgrāpayāmi I
Dhūpāṉantaram Ācamaṉīyam Samarpayāmi I

Śrī Dattātrēya Guravē Namaḥ Trivartti Dīpam Darśayāmi I
Dīpāṉantaram Ācamaṉīyam Samarpayāmi I

Śrī Dattātrēya Guravē Namaḥ Mahā Naivētyam Nivēdayāmi I
Naivēdyāṉantaram Ācamaṉīyam Samarpayāmi I

Madhyē Madhyē Pāṉīyam, Hasta Prakṣālaṉam, Pāda Prakṣālaṉam, Uttara Ācamaṉīyam Samarpayāmi I

Karpūra Tāmpūlam Samarpayāmi I

Oṃ Digambarāya Vidmahē Yōgīśvarāya Dīmahi I
Taṉṉō Datta Pracōtayāt I

Karpūra Nīrājaṉam Tarśayāmi I

Nīrājaṉāṉantaram Ācamaṉīyam Samarpayāmi I

Śrī Dattātrēya Guravē Namaḥ Mantra Puṣpam Samarpayāmi I

Aṉantakōṭi Pradakṣiṇa Namaskārāṉ Samarpayāmi I

Prārtaṉāṉ Samarpayāmi I

Samasta Rāja, Dēva Upacārāṉ Samarpayāmi I

Śrī Dattātrēya Guru Suprītaḥ Suprasaṉṉō Varadō Bavatu I

Pooja has to performed with shodasopachara, parayan Gurucharitra/ Datta mahatmyam/ datta puranam and Arghya should be given with the concerned mantras. After performing puja, naivedya and harathi to be performed. The item of Naivedya to be offered and Arghya mantras for each avathara may vary and also depends on the availability at the concerned location.

*****

Śrī Dattātreya Stotram

Note; This Stotram is told by Deva-sage Narada and is part of Narada Purana.

Jaṭādharaṃ Pāṇḍuraṅgaṃ Śūlahastaṃ Kṛpānidhim ।
(*Pāṇḍurāṅgaṃ*)
Sarvarogaharaṃ Devaṃ Dattātreyamahaṃ Bhaje ॥

Asya Śrīdattātreyastotramantrasya Bhagavān Nāradaṛṣiḥ ।
Anuṣṭup Chandaḥ । *Śrīdattaparamātmā Devatā* ।
Śrīdattaprītyarthe Jape Viniyogaḥ ॥

Jagadutpattikartre Ca Sthitisaṃhāra Hetave ।
Bhavapāśavimuktāya Dattātreya Namo'stute ॥ 1

Jarājanmavināśāya Dehaśuddhikarāya Ca ।
Digambaradayāmūrte Dattātreya Namo'stute ॥ 2

Karpūrakāntidehāya Brahmamūrtidharāya Ca ।
Vedaśāstraparijñāya Dattātreya Namo'stute ॥ 3

Hrasvadīrghakṛśasthūla-Nāmagotra-Vivarjita ।
Pañcabhūtaikadīptāya Dattātreya Namo'stute ॥ 4

Yajñabhokte Ca Yajñāya Yajñarūpadharāya Ca ।
Yajñapriyāya Siddhāya Dattātreya Namo'stute ॥ 5

Ādau Brahmā Madhya Viṣṇurante Devaḥ Sadāśivaḥ ।
Mūrtitrayasvarūpāya Dattātreya Namo'stute ॥ 6

Bhogālayāya Bhogāya Yogayogyāya Dhāriṇe ।
Jitendriyajitajñāya Dattātreya Namo'stute ॥ 7

Digambarāya Divyāya Divyarūpadharāya Ca ।
Sadoditaparabrahma Dattātreya Namo'stute ॥ 8

Jambudvīpamahākṣetramātāpuranivāsine ।
Jayamānasatāṃ Deva Dattātreya Namo'stute ॥ 9

Bhikṣāṭanaṃ Gṛhe Grāme Pātraṃ Hemamayaṃ Kare ।
Nānāsvādamayī Bhikṣā Dattātreya Namo'stute ।। 10

Brahmajñānamayī Mudrā Vastre Cākāśabhūtale ।
Prajñānaghanabodhāya Dattātreya Namo'stute ।। 11

Avadhūtasadānandaparabrahmasvarūpiṇe ।
Videhadeharūpāya Dattātreya Namo'stute ।। 12

Satyaṃrūpasadācārasatyadharmaparāyaṇa ।
Satyāśrayaparokṣāya Dattātreya Namo'stute ।। 13

Śūlahastagadāpāṇe Vanamālāsukandhara ।
Yajñasūtradharabrahman Dattātreya Namo'stute ।। 14

Kṣarākṣarasvarūpāya Parātparatarāya Ca ।
Dattamuktiparastotra Dattātreya Namo'stute ।। 15

Datta Vidyāḍhyalakṣmīśa Datta Svātmasvarūpiṇe ।
Guṇanirguṇarūpāya Dattātreya Namo'stute ।। 16

Śatrunāśakaraṃ Stotraṃ Jñānavijñānadāyakam ।
Sarvapāpaṃ Śamaṃ Yāti Dattātreya Namo'stute ।। 17

Idaṃ Stotraṃ Mahaddivyaṃ Dattapratyakṣakārakam ।
Dattātreyaprasādācca Nāradena Prakīrtitam ।। 18

Iti Śrīnārada Purāṇe Nārada Viracitaṃ Dattātreya Stotraṃ Susampūrṇam ।।

श्री दत्तात्रेय स्तोत्रम्

जटाधरं पाण्डुरङ्गं शूलहस्तं कृपानिधिम् । (पाण्डुराङ्गं)
सर्वरोगहरं देवं दत्तात्रेयमहं भजे ॥

अस्य श्रीदत्तात्रेयस्तोत्रमन्त्रस्य भगवान् नारदऋषिः ।
अनुष्टुप् छन्दः । श्रीदत्तपरमात्मा देवता । श्री दत्तप्रीत्यर्थे जपे विनियोगः ॥

जगदुत्पत्तिकर्त्रे च स्थितिसंहार हेतवे । भवपाशविमुक्ताय दत्तात्रेय नमोऽस्तुते ॥ १

जराजन्मविनाशाय देहशुद्धिकराय च । दिगम्बरदयामूर्ते दत्तात्रेय नमोऽस्तुते ॥ २

कर्पूरकान्तिदेहाय ब्रह्ममूर्तिधराय च । वेदशास्त्रपरिज्ञाय दत्तात्रेय नमोऽस्तुते ॥ ३

ह्रस्वदीर्घकृशस्थूल-नामगोत्र-विवर्जित । पञ्चभूतैकदीप्ताय दत्तात्रेय नमोऽस्तुते ॥ ४

यज्ञभोक्ते च यज्ञाय यज्ञरूपधराय च । यज्ञप्रियाय सिद्धाय दत्तात्रेय नमोऽस्तुते ॥ ५

आदौ ब्रह्मा मध्य विष्णुरन्ते देवः सदाशिवः । मूर्तित्रयस्वरूपाय दत्तात्रेय नमोऽस्तुते॥६

भोगालयाय भोगाय योगयोग्याय धारिणे । जितेन्द्रियजितज्ञाय दत्तात्रेय नमोऽस्तुते ॥७

दिगम्बराय दिव्याय दिव्यरूपधराय च । सदोदितपरब्रह्म दत्तात्रेय नमोऽस्तुते ॥ ८

जम्बुद्वीपमहाक्षेत्रमातापुरनिवासिने ।जयमानसतां देव दत्तात्रेय नमोऽस्तुते ॥ ९

भिक्षाटनं गृहे ग्रामे पात्रं हेममयं करे ।नानास्वादमयी भिक्षा दत्तात्रेय नमोऽस्तुते ॥ १०

ब्रह्मज्ञानमयी मुद्रा वस्त्रे चाकाशभूतले ।प्रज्ञानघनबोधाय दत्तात्रेय नमोऽस्तुते ॥ ११

अवधूतसदानन्दपरब्रह्मस्वरूपिणे । विदेहदेहरूपाय दत्तात्रेय नमोऽस्तुते ॥ १२

सत्यंरूपसदाचारसत्यधर्मपरायण । सत्याश्रयपरोक्षाय दत्तात्रेय नमोऽस्तुते ॥ १३

शूलहस्तगदापाणे वनमालासुकन्धर । यज्ञसूत्रधरब्रह्मन् दत्तात्रेय नमोऽस्तुते ॥ १४

क्षराक्षरस्वरूपाय परात्परतराय च । दत्तमुक्तिपरस्तोत्र दत्तात्रेय नमोऽस्तुते ॥ १५

दत्त विद्याढ्यलक्ष्मीश दत्त स्वात्मस्वरूपिणे । गुणनिर्गुणरूपाय दत्तात्रेय नमोऽस्तुते॥

शत्रुनाशकरं स्तोत्रं ज्ञानविज्ञानदायकम् ।सर्वपापं शमं याति दत्तात्रेय नमोऽस्तुते ॥ १७

इदं स्तोत्रं महद्दिव्यं दत्तप्रत्यक्षकारकम् ।दत्तात्रेयप्रसादाच्च नारदेन प्रकीर्तितम् ॥ १८

इति श्रीनारद पुराणे नारद विरचितं दत्तात्रेय स्तोत्रं सुसम्पूर्णम् ॥

Śrī Dattātreya Aṣṭa Cakrabīja Stotram

This Stotram is also called as "*Śrī Datta Ṣaṭcakra Stotram*" or "*Ajapā Japa Stotraṃ*". This stotram was recited by Srimad Shankaracharya in his book called "*Ajapa Tantra*".

Śrīgaṇeśāya Namaḥ I *Śrī Gurave Namaḥ* I

Dhyānam I

Digambaraṃ Bhasmasugandhalepanaṃ
Cakraṃ Triśūlaṃ Ḍamaruṃ Gadāṃ Ca I
Padmāsanasthaṃ Ṛṣidevavanditaṃ
Dattātreyadhyānamabhīṣṭasiddhidam I I

Oṃ Mūlādhāre Vārijapatre Caturasraṃ (Sacatuṣke)
Vaṃśaṃṣaṃsaṃ Varṇaviśālaṃ Suviśālam I
Raktaṃ Varṇaṃ Śrīgaṇanāthaṃ Bhagavantaṃ
Dattātreyaṃ Śrīgurūmūrtiṃ Praṇato'smi I I 1 *(Mūlādhāra)*

Svādhiṣṭhāne Ṣaṭdalapatre Tanuliṅge
Bālāntetadvarṇaviśālaṃ Suviśālam I
(Vādiṃ Lāntaṃ Varṇaviśeṣaṃ Suviśeṣam I*)*
Pītaṃ Varṇaṃ Vākpatiramaṇaṃ Druhiṇaṃ Taṃ
(Vākpatirūpaṃ, Duhilāntaṃ)
Dattātreyaṃ Śrīgurūmūrtiṃ Praṇato'smi I I 2 *(Svādhiṣṭhāna)*

Nābhaupadmaṃ Patradaśāṅkaṃ Ḍaphavarṇaṃ
(Nābhausthāne Patradaśābde)
Lakṣmīkāntaṃ Garuḍārūḍhaṃ Naravīram I *(Maṇipūre)*
Nīlaṃvarṇaṃ Nirguṇarūpaṃ Nigamāntaṃ (Nigamākṣaṃ)
Dattātreyaṃ Śrīgurūmūrtiṃ Praṇato'smi I I 3 *(Maṇipūra)*

Hṛtpadmāṃte Dvādaśapatre Kaḥ Varṇe (Kaṇṭhavarṇe)
Śambhośaivaṃ Pūrṇamayantaṃ Śaśivarṇam I
(Śambhośeśaṃ Jīvaviśeṣaṃ Smarayantam I*)*

(Sṛṣṭisthittaṃ Kuruvantaṃ Śivaśaktiṃ
Anāhatāṃte Vṛṣabhārūḍhaṃ Śivarūpam |)
Svargasthityaṃ Kuruvindūtaṃ Śivaśaktiṃ
(Kurvāṇaṃ Dhavalāṃgaṃ)
Dattātreyaṃ Śrīgurūmūrtiṃ Praṇato'smi || 4 (Anāhata)

Kaṇṭhasthāne Cakraviśuddhe Kamalānte
Candrākāre Ṣoḍaśapatre Svaravarṇe |
Māyādhīśaṃ Taijasarūpaṃ Bhagavaṃtaṃ
(Jīvaśivaṃ Taṃ Nijamūrtiṃ)
Dattātreyaṃ Śrīgurūmūrtiṃ Praṇato'smi || 5 (Viśuddha)

Ājñācakre Bhṛkuṭisthāne Dvidalānte (Agniścakre)
Haṃ Saṃ Bījaṃ Jñānasamudraṃ Gurūmūrtiḥ |
(Haṃ Kṣaṃ, Gurūmūrtiṃ)
Vidyutvarṇaṃ Jñānamayaṃ Taṃ Virupākṣaṃ (Niṭilākṣaṃ)
Dattātreyaṃ Śrīgurūmūrtiṃ Praṇato'smi || 6 (Ājñā)

Mūrdhnisthāne Vārijapatre Śaśibījaṃ
Śubhraṃ Varṇaṃ Patrasahasraṃ Suviśālam | (Lalanākhye |)
Haṃ Bījākhyaṃ Varṇasahasraṃ Turiyaṃ Taṃ (Turyāṃtaṃ)
Dattātreyaṃ Śrīgurūmūrtiṃ Praṇato'smi || 7 (Sahasrāra)

Brahmānandaṃ Brahmamukundaṃ Bhagavantaṃ
Brahmajñānaṃ Brahmamayaṃ Taṃ Svayamevam | (Jñānamayaṃ)
(Satyaṃ Jñānaṃ Satyamanantaṃ Bhagarūpam |)
Brahmātmānaṃ Brahmamunīdraṃ Bhasitābhaṃ
(Paramātmānaṃ Brahmamunīdraṃ Bhasitāṅgaṃ)
Dattātreyaṃ Śrīgurūmūrtiṃ Praṇato'smi || 8
(Pūrṇa Brahma Svarūpa)

Śāntākāraṃ Śeṣaśayānaṃ Suravandyaṃ
Kāntānāthaṃ Komalagātraṃ Kamalākṣam |
Cintāratnaṃ Cidghanapūrṇaṃ Dvijarājyaṃ (Dvijarājaṃ)
Dattātreyaṃ Śrīgurūmūrtiṃ Praṇato'smi || 9

Citaoṃkāraṃ Dhvaninãde Ca Svacchande

Ākārānte'kṣaravaṇīte Guṇarūpe I

Vedāntārthaṃ Jñānasvarūpaṃ Nijabodhaṃ

Dattātreyaṃ Śrīgurūmūrtiṃ Praṇato'smi II 10

Iti Śrī Ajapā Tantre Dattātreyas Stotraṃ Sampūrṇam I

Śubhaṃ Bhavatu I

Iti Śrīmad Śaṅkarācārya Viracitaṃ Śrī Dattātreya Aṣṭacakrabīja Stotraṃ Sampūrṇam I

श्रीदत्तात्रेय अष्ट चक्रबीजस्तोत्रम्

श्रीदत्त षट्चक्रस्तोत्रम् अजपाजप स्तोत्रं च।

श्रीगणेशाय नमः। श्री गुरवे नमः।

अथ ध्यानम्।

दिगम्बरं भस्मसुगन्धलेपनंचक्रं त्रिशूलं डमरुं गदां च।
पद्मासनस्थं ऋषिदेववन्दितं दत्तात्रेयध्यानमभीष्टसिद्धिदम्॥

ॐ मूलाधारे वारिजपत्रे चतुरस्रं (सचतुष्के) वंशंषंसं वर्णविशालं सुविशालम्।
रक्तं वर्णं श्रीगणनाथं भगवन्तं दत्तात्रेयं श्रीगुरूमूर्तिं प्रणतोऽस्मि॥ १ (मूलाधार)

स्वाधिष्ठाने षट्दलपत्रे तनुलिङ्गेबालान्तेतद्वर्णविशालं सुविशालम्।
(वादिं लान्तं वर्णविशेषं सुविशेषम्।)
पीतं वर्णं वाक्पतिरमणं द्रुहिणं तं (वाक्पतिरूपंदुहिलान्तं)
दत्तात्रेयं श्रीगुरूमूर्तिं प्रणतोऽस्मि॥ २ (स्वाधिष्ठान)

नाभौपद्मं पत्रदशाङ्कं डफवर्णं (नाभौस्थाने पत्रदशाब्दे)
लक्ष्मीकान्तं गरुडारूढं नरवीरम्। (मणिपूरे।)
नीलंवर्णं निर्गुणरूपं निगमान्तं (निगमाक्षंदत्तात्रेयं श्रीगुरूमूर्तिं प्रणतोऽस्मि॥ ३
(मणिपूर)

हृत्पद्मांते द्वादशपत्रे कः वर्णे (कण्ठवर्णे)
शम्भोशैवं पूर्णमयन्तं शशिवर्णम्। (शम्भोशेशं जीवविशेषं स्मरयन्तम्।)

(सृष्टिस्थित्तं कुरुवन्तं शिवशक्तिं अनाहतांते वृषभारूढं शिवरूपम् ।)
स्वर्गस्थित्यं कुरुविन्दूतं शिवशक्तिं (कुर्वाणं धवलांगं)
दत्तात्रेयं श्रीगुरूमूर्तिं प्रणतोऽस्मि ॥ ४ (अनाहत)

कण्ठस्थाने चक्रविशुद्धे कमलान्ते चन्द्राकारे षोडशपत्रे स्वरवर्णे ।
मायाधीशं तैजसरूपं भगवंतं (जीवशिवं तं निजमूर्तिं)
दत्तात्रेयं श्रीगुरूमूर्तिं प्रणतोऽस्मि ॥ ५ (विशुद्ध)

आज्ञाचक्रे भृकुटिस्थाने द्विदलान्ते (अग्निश्चक्रे)
हं सं बीजं ज्ञानसमुद्रं गुरूमूर्तिः । (हं क्षंगुरूमूर्तिं)
विद्युत्वर्णं ज्ञानमयं तं विरुपाक्षं (निटिलाक्षं)
दत्तात्रेयं श्रीगुरूमूर्तिं प्रणतोऽस्मि ॥ ६ (आज्ञा)

मूर्ध्निस्थाने वारिजपत्रे शशिबीजं
शुभ्रं वर्णं पत्रसहस्रं सुविशालम् । (ललनाख्ये ।)
हं बीजाख्यं वर्णसहस्रं तुरियं तं (तुर्यांतं)
दत्तात्रेयं श्रीगुरूमूर्तिं प्रणतोऽस्मि ॥ ७ (सहस्रार)

ब्रह्मानन्दं ब्रह्ममुकुन्दं भगवन्तं
ब्रह्मज्ञानं ब्रह्ममयं तं स्वयमेवम् । (ज्ञानमयं)
(सत्यं ज्ञानं सत्यमनन्तं भगरूपम् ।)
ब्रह्मात्मानं ब्रह्ममुनीद्रं भसिताभं (परमात्मानं ब्रह्ममुनीद्रं भसिताङ्गं)
दत्तात्रेयं श्रीगुरूमूर्तिं प्रणतोऽस्मि ॥ ८ (पूर्णब्रह्मस्वरूप)

शान्ताकारं शेषशयानं सुरवन्द्यंकान्तानाथं कोमलगात्रं कमलाक्षम् ।
चिन्तारत्नं चिद्धनपूर्णं द्विजराज्यं (द्विजराजं)दत्तात्रेयं श्रीगुरूमूर्तिं प्रणतोऽस्मि ॥ ९

चितओंकारं ध्वनिनादे च स्वच्छन्दे आकारान्तेऽक्षरवणीते गुणरूपे ।
वेदान्तार्थं ज्ञानस्वरूपं निजबोधं दत्तात्रेयं श्रीगुरूमूर्तिं प्रणतोऽस्मि ॥ १०

इति श्री अजपा तन्त्रे दत्तात्रेय स्तोत्रं सम्पूर्णम् । शुभं भवतु ।

(इति श्रीमद्श ङ्कराचार्य विरचितं श्रीदत्तात्रेय अष्ट चक्रबीज स्तोत्रं सम्पूर्णम् ।)

*****

Śrī Dattātreya Dvādaśa Nāma Stotram

This Stotram details the 12 names of *Śrī Dattātreya.*

Śrī Gaṇeśāya Namaḥ ।

Asya Śrī Dattātreya Gvādaśanāma Stotra Mantrasya
Paramahaṃsa Ṛṣiḥ ।
Śrīdattātreya Paramātmā Devatā । *Anuṣṭupchandaḥ* ।
Sakala kKāmanā Siddhyarthe Jape Viniyogaḥ ।

Prathamastu Mahāyogī Dvitīyaḥ Prabhurīśvaraḥ ।
Tṛtīyaśca Trimūrtiśca Caturtho Jñānasāgaraḥ ।। 1

Pañcamo Jñānavijñānaṃ Ṣaṣṭhaḥsyāt Sarvamaṅgalam ।
Saptamaḥ Puṇḍarīkākṣo Aṣṭamo Devavallabhaḥ ।। 2

Navamo Nandadeveśo Daśamo Nandadāyakaḥ ।
Ekādaśo Mahārudraḥ Dvādaśaḥ Karuṇākaraḥ ।। 3

Etāni Dvādaśanāmāni Dattātreya Mahātmanaḥ ।
Mantrarājeti Vikhyātaṃ Dattātreya Haraḥ Parāḥ ।। 4

Kṣayopasmāra Kuṣṭhādi Tāpajvaranivāraṇam ।
Rājadvāre Pathe'ghore Saṅgrāmeṣu Jalāntare ।। 5

Gire Gṛhāntare'raṇye Vyāghracorabhayādiṣu ।
Āvartane Sahasreṣu Labhante Vāñchitaṃ Phalam ।। 6

Trikālaṃ Yaḥ Paṭhennityaṃ Mokṣasiddhimavāpnuyāt ।
Dattātreya Sadā Rakṣedyaśaḥ Satyaṃ Na Saṃśayaḥ ।। 7

Vidyārthī Labhate Vidyāṃ Rogī Rogāt Pramucyate ।
Aputro Labhate Putraṃ Daridro Labhate Dhanam ।। 8

Abhāryo Labhate Bhāryāṃ Sukhārthī Labhate Sukham ।
Mucyate Sarvapāpebhyo Sarvatra Vijayī Bhavet ।। 9

Iti Śrī Dattātreya Dvādaśa Nāma Stotraṃ Sampūrṇam ।।
Śrī Dattātreyārpaṇamastu ।।

श्री दत्तात्रेय द्वादश नाम स्तोत्रम् ।

श्री गणेशाय नमः ।

अस्य श्री दत्तात्रेय द्वादशनाम स्तोत्रमन्त्रस्य परमहंस ऋषिः ।
श्रीदत्तात्रेय परमात्मा देवता । अनुष्टुप्छन्दः ।
सकलकामनासिद्ध्यर्थे जपे विनियोगः ।

प्रथमस्तु महायोगी द्वितीयः प्रभुरीश्वरः ।तृतीयश्च त्रिमूर्तिश्च चतुर्थो ज्ञानसागरः ॥ १

पञ्चमो ज्ञानविज्ञानं षष्ठःस्यात् सर्वमङ्गलम् ।
सप्तमः पुण्डरीकाक्षो अष्टमो देववल्लभः ॥ २

नवमो नन्ददेवेशो दशमो नन्ददायकः । एकादशो महारुद्रः द्वादशः करुणाकरः ॥ ३

एतानि द्वादशनामानि दत्तात्रेय महात्मनः ।
मन्त्रराजेति विख्यातं दत्तात्रेय हरः पराः ॥ ४

क्षयोपस्मार कुष्ठादि तापज्वरनिवारणम् । राजद्वारे पथेऽघोरे सङ्ग्रामेषु जलान्तरे ॥ ५॥

गिरे गृहान्तरेऽरण्ये व्याघ्रचोरभयादिषु ।
आवर्तने सहस्रेषु लभन्ते वाञ्छितं फलम् ॥ ६

त्रिकालं यः पठेन्नित्यं मोक्षसिद्धिमवाप्नुयात् ।
दत्तात्रेय सदा रक्षेद्यशः सत्यं न संशयः ॥ ७

विद्यार्थी लभते विद्यां रोगी रोगात् प्रमुच्यते ।
अपुत्रो लभते पुत्रं दरिद्रो लभते धनम् ॥ ८

अभार्यो लभते भार्यां सुखार्थी लभते सुखम् ।
मुच्यते सर्वपापेभ्यो सर्वत्र विजयी भवेत् ॥ ९

इति श्री दत्तात्रेय द्वादश नाम स्तोत्रं
सम्पूर्णम् ॥

श्री दत्तात्रेयार्पणमस्तु ॥

*****

Śrī Dattātreya Vajra Kavacam

Generally Kavacam means shield. Vajra Kavacam is a thunderbolt – very strong shield. This Stotram is a shield not for the outside body, but for the inner-self, like Skanda Shashti Kavacam, Sri Devi Kavacam, and so on. This is part of *Śrī Rudra Yāmala* tantra text as a dialogue between *Umā* and *Maheśvara*.

Śrī Dattātreya Vajra Kavaca Stotraṃ

Śrī Gaṇeśāya Namaḥ । *Śrī Dattātreyāya Namaḥ* ।

Ṛṣaya Ūcuḥ ।

Kathaṃ Saṅkalpasiddhiḥ Syādvedavyāsa Kalau Yuge ।
Dharmārthakāmamokṣāṇāṃ Sādhanaṃ Kimudāhṛtam ।। 1

Vyāsa Uvāca ।

Śṛṇvanturṣayaḥ Sarve Śīghraṃ Saṅkalpasādhanam ।
Sakṛduccāramātreṇa Bhogamokṣapradāyakam ।। 2

Gaurīśṛṅge Himavataḥ Kalpavṛkṣopaśobhitam ।
Dīpte Divyamahāratnahemamaṇḍapamadhyagam ।। 3

Ratnasiṃhāsanāsinaṃ Prasannaṃ Parameśvaram ।
Mandasmitamukhāmbhojaṃ Śaṅkaraṃ Prāha Pārvatī ।। 4

Śrī Devyuvāca ।

Devadeva Mahādeva Lokaśaṅkara Śaṅkara ।
Mantrajālāni Sarvāṇi Yantrajālāni Kṛtsnaśaḥ ।। 5

Tantrajālānyanekāni Mayā Tvattaḥ Śrutāni Vai ।
Idānīṃ Draṣṭumicchāmi Viśeṣeṇa Mahītalam ।। 6

Ityudīritamākarṇya Pārvatyā Parameśvaraḥ ।
Kareṇāmṛjya Santoṣātpārvatīṃ Pratyabhāṣata ।। 7

Mayedānīṃ Tvayā Sārdhaṃ Vṛṣamāruhya Gamyate ।

Ityuktvā Vṛṣamāruhya Pārvatyā Saha Śaṅkaraḥ || 8

Yayau Bhūmaṇḍalaṃ Draṣṭuṃ Gauryāścitrāṇi Darśayan |
Kvacit Vindhyācalaprānte Mahāraṇye Sudurgame || 9

Tatra Vyāhartumāyāntaṃ Bhillaṃ Paraśudhāriṇam |
Vardhyamānaṃ Mahāvyāghraṃ Nakhadaṃṣṭrābhirāvṛtam || 10

Atīva Citracāritryaṃ Vajrakāyasamāyutam |
Aprayatnamanāyāsamakhilaṃ Sukhamāsthitam || 11

Palāyantaṃ Mṛgaṃ Paścādvyāghro Bhītyā Palāyitaḥ |
Etadāścaryamālokya Pārvatī Prāha Śaṅkaram || 12

Śrī Pārvatyuvāca |

Kimāścaryaṃ Kimāścaryamagre Śambho Nirīkṣyatām |
Ityuktaḥ Sa Tataḥ Śambhurdṛṣṭvā Prāha Purāṇavit || 13

Śrī Śaṅkara Uvāca |

Gauri Vakṣyāmi Te Citramavāṅmānasagocaram |
Adṛṣṭapūrvamasmābhirnāsti Kiñcanna Kutracit || 14

Mayā Samyak Samāsena Vakṣyate Śṛṇu Pārvati |
Ayaṃ Dūraśravā Nāma Bhillaḥ Paramadhārmikaḥ || 15

Samitkuśaprasūnāni Kandamūlaphalādikam |
Pratyahaṃ Vipinaṃ Gatvā Samādāya Prayāsataḥ || 16

Priye Pūrvaṃ Munīndrebhyaḥ Prayacchati Na Vāñchati |
Te'pi Tasminnapi Dayāṃ Kurvate Sarvamauninaḥ || 17

Dalādano Mahāyogī Vasanneva Nijāśrame |
Kadācidasmarat Siddhaṃ Dattātreyaṃ Digambaram || 18

Dattātreyaḥ Smartṛgāmī Cetihāsaṃ Parīkṣitum |
Tatkṣaṇātso'pi Yogīndro Dattātreyaḥ Samutthitaḥ || 19

Taṃ Dṛṣṭvā''ścaryatoṣābhyāṃ Dalādanamahāmuniḥ |

Sampūjyāgre Niṣīdantaṃ Dattātreyamuvāca Tam ।। 20

Mayopahūtaḥ Samprāpto Dattātreya Mahāmune ।
Smartṛgāmī Tvamityetat Kiṃvadantī Parīkṣitum ।। 21

Mayādya Saṃsmṛto'si Tvamaparādhaṃ Kṣamasva Me ।
Dattātreyo Muniṃ Prāha Mama Prakṛtirīdṛśī ।। 22

Abhaktyā Vā Subhaktyā Vā Yaḥ Smarenmāmananyadhīḥ ।
Tadānīṃ Tamupāgatya Dadāmi Tadabhīpsitam ।। 23

Dattātreyo Muniṃ Prāha Dalādanamunīśvaram ।
Yadiṣṭaṃ Tadvṛṇīṣva Tvaṃ Yat Prāpto'haṃ Tvayā Smṛtaḥ ।। 24

Dattātreyaṃ Muniḥ Prāha Mayā Kimapi Nocyate ।
Tvaccitte Yatsthitaṃ Tanme Prayaccha Munipuṅgava ।। 25

Śrī Dattātreya Uvāca ।

Mamāsti Vajrakavacaṃ Gṛhāṇetyavadanmunim ।
Tathyetyaṅgīkṛtavate Dalādanamunaye Muniḥ ।। 26

Svavajrakavacaṃ Prāha Ṛṣicchandaḥpuraḥsaram ।
Nyāsaṃ Dhyānaṃ Phalaṃ Tatra Prayojanamaśeṣataḥ ।। 27

Asya Śrī Dattātreya Vajra Kavaca Stotra Mantrasya,
Kirātarūpī Mahārudra Ṛṣiḥ, Anuṣṭup Chandaḥ,
Śrīdattātreyo Devatā, Drāṃ Bījaṃ, Āṃ Śaktiḥ,
Krauṃ Kīlakaṃ, Oṃ Ātmane Namaḥ । *Oṃ Drīṃ Manase Namaḥ* ।
Oṃ Āṃ Drīṃ Śrīṃ Sauḥ Oṃ Klāṃ Klīṃ Klūṃ Klaiṃ Klauṃ Klaḥ ।
Śrī Dattātreya Prasāda Siddhyarthe Jape Viniyogaḥ ।।

Karanyāsaḥ ।

Oṃ Drāṃ Aṅguṣṭhābhyāṃ Namaḥ ।
Oṃ Drīṃ Tarjanībhyāṃ Namaḥ ।
Oṃ Drūṃ Madhyamābhyāṃ Namaḥ ।
Oṃ Draiṃ Anāmikābhyāṃ Namaḥ ।
Oṃ Drauṃ Kaniṣṭhikābhyāṃ Namaḥ ।

Oṃ Draḥ Karatalakarapṛṣṭhābhyāṃ Namaḥ ।।

Hṛdayādinyāsaḥ ।

Oṃ Drāṃ Hṛdayāya Namaḥ ।
Oṃ Drīṃ Śirase Svāhā ।
Oṃ Drūṃ Śikhāyai Vaṣaṭ ।
Oṃ Draiṃ Kavacāya Huṃ ।
Oṃ Drauṃ Netratrayāya Vauṣaṭ ।
Oṃ Draḥ Astrāya Phaṭ ।
Oṃ Bhūrbhuvaḥsvaromiti Digbandhaḥ ।।

Dhyānam ।

Jagadaṅkurakandāya Saccidānandamūrtaye ।
Dattātreyāya Yogīndracandrāya Paramātmane ।। 1

Kadā Yogī Kadā Bhogī Kadā Nagnaḥ Piśācavat ।
Dattātreyo Hariḥ Sākṣādbhuktimuktipradāyakaḥ ।। 2

Vārāṇasīpurasnāyī Kolhāpurajapādaraḥ ।
Māhurīpurabhikṣāśī Sahyaśāyī Digambara ।। 3

Indranīlasamākāraścandrakāntisamadyutiḥ ।
Vaiḍuryasadṛśasphūrtiścalatkiñcijjaṭādharaḥ ।। 4

Snigdhadhāvalyayuktākṣo'tyantanīlakanīnikaḥ ।
Bhrūvakṣaḥśmaśrunīlāṅkaḥ Saśāṅkasadṛśānanaḥ ।। 5

Hāsanirjitanīhāraḥ Kaṇṭhanirjitakambukaḥ ।
Māṃsalāṃso Dīrghabāhuḥ Pāṇinirjitapallavaḥ ।। 6

Viśālapīnavakṣāśca Tāmrapāṇirdalodaraḥ ।
Pṛthulaśroṇilalito Viśālajaghanasthalaḥ ।। 7

Rambhāstambhopamānorurjānupūrvaikajaṅghakaḥ ।
Gūḍhagulphaḥ Kūrmapṛṣṭholasatpādoṣaristhalaḥ ।। 8

Raktāravindasadṛśaramaṇīyapadādharaḥ ।

Carmāmbaradharo Yogī Smartṛgāmī Kṣaṇe Kṣaṇe ।। 9

Jñānopadeśanīrato Vipaddharaṇadīkṣitaḥ ।
Siddhāsanasamāsīna Ṛjukāyo Hasanmukhaḥ ।। 10

Vāmahastena Varado Dakṣiṇenābhayaṅkaraḥ ।
Bālonmattapiśācībhiḥ Kvacidyuktaḥ Parīkṣitaḥ ।। 11

Tyāgī Bhogī Mahāyogī Nityānando Nirañjanaḥ ।
Sarvarūpī Sarvadātā Sarvagaḥ Sarvakāmadaḥ ।। 12

Bhasmoddhūlitasarvāṅgo Mahāpātakanāśanaḥ ।
Bhuktiprado Muktidātā Jīvanmukto Na Saṃśayaḥ ।। 13

Evaṃ Dhyātvā'nanyacitto Madvajrakavacaṃ Paṭhet ।
Māmeva Paśyansarvatra Sa Mayā Saha Saṅcaret ।। 14

Digambaraṃ Bhasmasugandhalepanaṃ Cakraṃ Triśūlaṃ
Ḍamaruṃ Gadāyudham ।
Padmāsanaṃ Yogimunīndravanditaṃ Datteti Nāmasmaraṇena
Nityam ।। 15

Atha Pañcopacāraiḥ Saṃpūjya Oṃ Drāṃ Iti Aṣṭottaraśatavāraṃ Japet

Note; Do Panca Puja and chant "*Oṃ Drāṃ*" Moola Mantra 108 times.

Oṃ Drām ।

Kavacam ।

Oṃ Dattātreyaḥ Śiraḥ Pātu Sahasrābjeṣu Saṃsthitaḥ ।
Bhālaṃ Pātvānasūyeyaścandramaṇḍalamadhyagaḥ ।। 1

Kūrcaṃ Manomayaḥ Pātu Haṃ Kṣaṃ Dvidalapadmabhūḥ ।
Jyotirūpo'kṣiṇī Pātu Pātu Śabdātmakaḥ Śrutī ।। 2

Nāsikāṃ Pātu Gandhātmā Mukhaṃ Pātu Rasātmakaḥ ।
Jihvāṃ Vedātmakaḥ Pātu Dantoṣṭhau Pātu Dhārmikaḥ ।। 3

Kapolāvatribhūḥ Pātu Pātvaśeṣaṃ Mamātvavit ।

Svarātmā Ṣoḍaśārābjasthitaḥ Svātmā'vatādgalam || 4

Skandhau Çandrānujaḥ Pātu Bhujau Pātu Kṛtādibhūḥ |
Jatruṇī Śatrujit Pātu Pātu Vakṣaḥsthalaṃ Hariḥ || 5

Kādiṭhāntadvādaśārapadmago Marudātmakaḥ |
Yogīśvareśvaraḥ Pātu Hṛdayaṃ Hṛdayasthitaḥ || 6

Pārśve Hariḥ Pārśvavartī Pātu Pārśvasthitaḥ Smṛtaḥ |
Haṭhayogādiyogajñaḥ Kukṣī Pātu Kṛpānidhiḥ || 7

Ḍakārādiphakārāntadaśārasarasīruhe |
Nābhisthale Vartamāno Nābhiṃ Vahnyātmako'vatu || 8

Vahnitatvamayo Yogī Rakṣatānmaṇipūrakam |
Kaṭiṃ Kaṭisthabrahmāṇḍavāsudevātmako'vatu || 9

Bakārādilakārāntaṣaṭpatrāmbujabodhakaḥ | *(Vakrādi)*
Jalatatvamayo Yogī Svādhiṣṭhānaṃ Mamāvatu || 10

Siddhāsanasamāsīna Ūrū Siddheśvaro'vatu |
Vādisāntacatuṣpatrasaroruhanibodhakaḥ || 11

Mūlādhāraṃ Mahīrūpo Rakṣatādvīryanigrahī |
Pṛṣṭhaṃ Ca Sarvataḥ Pātu Jānyunyastakarāmbujaḥ || 12

Jaṅghe Pātvavadhūtendraḥ Pātvaṅghrī Tīrthapāvanaḥ |
Sarvāṅgaṃ Pātu Sarvātmā Romāṇyavatu Keśavaḥ || 13

Carma Carmāmbaraḥ Pātu Raktaṃ Bhaktipriyo'vatu |
Māṃsaṃ Māṃsakaraḥ Pātu Majjāṃ Majjātmako'vatu || 14

Asthīni Sthiradhīḥ Pāyānmedhāṃ Vedhāḥ Prapālayet |
Śukraṃ Sukhakaraḥ Pātu Cittaṃ Pātu Dṛḍhākṛtiḥ || 15

Manobuddhimahaṅkāraṃ Hṛṣīkeśātmako'vatu |
Karmendriyāṇi Pātvīśaḥ Pātu Jñānendriyāṇyajaḥ || 16

Bandhūn Bandhūttamaḥ Pāyācchatrubhyaḥ Pātu Śatrujit |
Gṛhārāmadhanakṣetraputrādīñchaṅkaro'vatu || 17

Bhāryāṃ Prakṛtivit Pātu Paśvādīnpātu Śārṅgabhṛt ।
Prāṇānpātu Pradhānajño Bhakṣyādīnpātu Bhāskaraḥ ।। 18

Sukhaṃ Candrātmakaḥ Pātu Duḥkhāt Pātu Purāntakaḥ ।
Paśūnpaśūpatiḥ Pātu Bhūtiṃ Bhūteśvaro Mama ।। 19

Prācyāṃ Viṣaharaḥ Pātu Pātvāgneyyāṃ Makhātmakaḥ ।
Yāmyāṃ Dharmātmakaḥ Pātu Nairṛtyāṃ Sarvavairihṛt ।। 20

Varāhaḥ Pātu Vāruṇyāṃ Vāyavyāṃ Prāṇado'vatu ।
Kauberyāṃ Dhanadaḥ Pātu Pātvaiśānyāṃ Mahāguruḥ ।। 21

Urdhvaṃ Pātu Mahāsiddhaḥ Pātvadhastājjaṭādharaḥ ।
Rakṣāhīnaṃ Tu Yatsthānaṃ Rakṣatvādimunīśvaraḥ ।। 22

Oṃ Drām । *Mālāmantrajapaḥ* । (*Punaḥ* - again)

Karanyāsaḥ ।

Oṃ Drāṃ Aṅguṣṭhābhyāṃ Namaḥ ।
Oṃ Drīṃ Tarjanībhyāṃ Namaḥ ।
Oṃ Drūṃ Madhyamābhyāṃ Namaḥ ।
Oṃ Draiṃ Anāmikābhyāṃ Namaḥ ।
Oṃ Drauṃ Kaniṣṭhikābhyāṃ Namaḥ ।
Oṃ Draḥ Karatalakarapṛṣṭhābhyāṃ Namaḥ ।।

Hṛdayādinyāsaḥ ।

Oṃ Drāṃ Hṛdayāya Namaḥ ।
Oṃ Drīṃ Śirase Svāhā ।
Oṃ Drūṃ Śikhāyai Vaṣaṭ ।
Oṃ Draiṃ Kavacāya Huṃ ।
Oṃ Drauṃ Netratrayāya Vauṣaṭ ।
Oṃ Draḥ Astrāya Phaṭ ।
Oṃ Bhūrbhuvaḥsvaromiti Digbandhaḥ ।।

Etanme Vajrakavacaṃ Yaḥ Paṭhecchṛṇuyādapi ।
Vajrakāyaścirañjīvī Dattātreyo'hamabruvam ।। 23

Tyāgī Bhogī Mahāyogī Sukhaduḥkhavivarjitaḥ ।
Sarvatrasiddhasaṅkalpo Jīvanmukto'dya Vartate ॥ 24

Ityuktvāntardadhe Yogī Dattātreyo Digambaraḥ ।
Dalādano'pi Tajjaptvā Jīvanmuktaḥ Sa Vartate ॥ 25

Bhillo Dūraśravā Nāma Tadānīṃ Śrutavādinam ।
Sakṛcchravaṇamātreṇa Vajrāṅgo'bhavadapyasau ॥ 26

Ityetadvajrakavacaṃ Dattātreyasya Yoginaḥ ।
Śrutvāśeṣaṃ Śambhumukhāt Punarapyāha Pārvatī ॥ 27

Pārvatyuvāca ।

Etatkavacamāhātmyaṃ Vada Vistarato Mama ।
Kutra Kena Kadā Jāpyaṃ Kiṃ Yajāpyaṃ Kathaṃ Katham ॥ 28

Uvāca Śambhustatsarvaṃ Pārvatyā Vinayoditam ।

Śrī Śiva Uvāca ।

Śruṇu Pārvati Vakṣyāmi Samāhitamanāvilam ॥ 29

Dharmārthakāmamokṣāṇāmidameva Parāyaṇam ।
Hastyaśvarathapādātisarvaiśvaryapradāyakam ॥ 30

Putramitrakalatrādisarvasantoṣasādhanam ।
Vedaśāstrādividyānāṃ Nidhānaṃ Paramaṃ Hi Tat ॥ 31

Saṅgītaśāstrasāhityasatkavitvavidhāyakam ।
Buddhividyāsmṛtiprajñāmatiprauḍhipradāyakam ॥ 32

Sarvasantoṣakaraṇaṃ Sarvaduḥkhanivāraṇam ।
Śatru Saṃhārakaṃ Śīghraṃ Yaśaḥkīrtivivardhanam ॥ 33

Aṣṭasaṃkhyā Mahārogāḥ Sannipātāstrayodaśa ।
Ṣaṇṇavatyakṣirogāśca Viṃśatirmeharogakāḥ ॥ 34

Aṣṭādaśa Tu Kuṣṭhāni Gulmānyaṣṭavidhānyapi ।
Aśītirvātarogāśca Catvāriśattu Paittikāḥ ॥ 35

Viṃśatiśleṣmarogāśca Kṣayacāturthikādayaḥ ।
Mantrayantrakuyogādyāḥ Kalpatantrādinirmitāḥ ।। 36

Brahmarākṣasavetālakūṣmāṇḍādigrahodbhavāḥ ।
Saṅgajāḥ Deśakālasthāstāpatrayasamutthitāḥ ।। 37

Navagrahasamudbhūtā Mahāpātakasambhavāḥ ।
Sarve Rogāḥ Praṇaśyanti Sahasrāvartanāddhruvam ।। 38

Ayutāvṛttimātreṇa Vandhyā Putravatī Bhavet ।
Ayutadvitayāvṛttyā Hyapamṛtyujayo Bhavet ।। 39

Ayutatritayāccaiva Khecaratvaṃ Prajāyate ।
Sahasrādayutādarvāk Sarvakāryāṇi Sādhayet ।। 40

Lakṣāvṛtyā Kāryasiddhirbhavetyeva Na Saṃśayaḥ ।। 41

Viṣavṛkṣasya Mūleṣu Tiṣṭhan Vai Dakṣiṇāmukhaḥ ।
Kurute Māsamātreṇa Vairiṇaṃ Vikalendriyam ।। 42

Audumbaratarormūle Vṛddhikāmena Jāpyate ।
Śrīvakṣamūle Śrīkāmī Tintiṇī Śāntikarmaṇi ।। 43

Ojaskāmo'śvatthamūle Strīkāmaiḥ Sahakārake ।
Jñānārthī Tulasīmūle Garbhagehe Sutārthibhiḥ ।। 44

Dhanārthibhistu Sukṣetre Paśukāmaistu Goṣṭhake ।
Devālaye Sarvakāmaistatkāle Sarvadarśitam ।। 45

Nābhimātrajale Sthitvā Bhānumālokya Yo Japet ।
Yuddhe Vā Śāstravāde Vā Sahasreṇa Jayo Bhavet ।। 46

Kaṇṭhamātre Jale Sthitvā Yo Rātrau Kavacaṃ Paṭhet ।
Jvarāpasmārakuṣṭhāditāpajvaranivāraṇam ।। 47

Yatra Yatsyātsthiraṃ Yadyatprasannaṃ Tannivartate ।
Tena Tatra Hi Japtavyaṃ Tataḥ Siddhirbhaveddhruvam ।। 48

Ityuktvān Ca Śivo Gaurye Rahasyaṃ Paramaṃ Śubham ।
Yaḥ Paṭhet Vajrakavacaṃ Dattātreyosamo Bhavet ।। 49

Evaṃ Śivena Kathitaṃ Himavatsutāyai
Proktaṃ Dalādamunaye'trisutenapūrvam ।
Yaḥ Ko'pi Vajrakavacaṃ Paṭhatīha Loke
Dattopamaścarati Yogivaraścirāyuḥ ।। 50

Iti Śrī Rudra Yāmale Himavat Khaṇḍe Mantra Śāstre Upāsanā Khaṇḍe Śiva Vijaya Siddhānte Umā Maheśvara Saṃvāde Śrī Dattātreya Vajra Kavaca Stotraṃ Sampūrṇam ।।

Śrī Dattātreyārpaṇamastu ।

श्री दत्तात्रेय वज्र कवचम् ।

श्री गणेशाय नमः । श्री दत्तात्रेयाय नमः ।

ऋषय ऊचुः ।

कथं सङ्कल्पसिद्धिः स्याद्वेदव्यास कलौ युगे ।
धर्मार्थकाममोक्षाणां साधनं किमुदाहृतम् ॥ १

व्यास उवाच ।

शृण्वन्तुऋषयः सर्वे शीघ्रं सङ्कल्पसाधनम् ।
सकृदुच्चारमात्रेण भोगमोक्षप्रदायकम् ॥

गौरीशृङ्गे हिमवतः कल्पवृक्षोपशोभितम् ।
दीप्ते दिव्यमहारत्नहेममण्डपमध्यगम् ॥

रत्नसिंहासनासिनं प्रसन्नं परमेश्वरम् ।
मन्दस्मितमुखाम्भोजं शङ्करं प्राह पार्वती ॥

श्री देव्युवाच ।

देवदेव महादेव लोकशङ्कर शङ्कर ।
मन्त्रजालानि सर्वाणि यन्त्रजालानि कृत्स्नशः ॥ ५

तन्त्रजालान्यनेकानि मया त्वत्तः श्रुतानि वै ।
इदानीं द्रष्टुमिच्छामि विशेषेण महीतलम् ॥ ६

इत्युदीरितमाकर्ण्य पार्वत्या परमेश्वरः ।
करेणामृज्य सन्तोषात्पार्वतीं प्रत्यभाषत ॥ ७

मयेदानीं त्वया सार्धं वृषमारुह्य गम्यते ।
इत्युक्त्वा वृषमारुह्य पार्वत्या सह शङ्करः ॥ ८

ययौ भूमण्डलं द्रष्टुं गौर्याश्चित्राणि दर्शयन् ।
क्वचित् विन्ध्याचलप्रान्ते महारण्ये सुदुर्गमे ॥ ९

तत्र व्याहर्तुमायान्तं भिल्लं परशुधारिणम् ।
वर्ध्यमानं महाव्याघ्रं नखदंष्ट्राभिरावृतम् ॥ १०

अतीव चित्रचारित्र्यं वज्रकायसमायुतम् ।
अप्रयत्नमनायासमखिलं सुखमास्थितम् ॥ ११

पलायन्तं मृगं पश्चाद्व्याघ्रो भीत्या पलायितः ।
एतदाश्चर्यमालोक्य पार्वती प्राह शङ्करम् ॥ १२

श्रीपार्वत्युवाच ।

किमाश्चर्यं किमाश्चर्यमग्रे शम्भो निरीक्ष्यताम् ।
इत्युक्तः स ततः शम्भुर्दृष्ट्वा प्राह पुराणवित् ॥ १३

श्रीशङ्कर उवाच ।

गौरि वक्ष्यामि ते चित्रमवाङ्मानसगोचरम् ।
अदृष्टपूर्वमस्माभिर्नास्ति किञ्चन्न कुत्रचित् ॥ १४

मया सम्यक् समासेन वक्ष्यते शृणु पार्वति ।
अयं दूरश्रवा नाम भिल्लः परमधार्मिकः ॥ १५

समित्कुशप्रसूनानि कन्दमूलफलादिकम् ।
प्रत्यहं विपिनं गत्वा समादाय प्रयासतः ॥ १६

प्रिये पूर्वं मुनीन्द्रेभ्यः प्रयच्छति न वाञ्छति ।
तेऽपि तस्मिन्नपि दयां कुर्वते सर्वमौनिनः ॥ १७

दलादनो महायोगी वसन्नेव निजाश्रमे ।

कदाचिदस्मरत् सिद्धं दत्तात्रेयं दिगम्बरम् ॥ १८

दत्तात्रेयः स्मर्तृगामी चेतिहासं परीक्षितुम् ।
तत्क्षणात्सोऽपि योगीन्द्रो दत्तात्रेयः समुत्थितः ॥ १९

तं दृष्ट्वाऽऽश्चर्यतोषाभ्यां दलादनमहामुनिः ।
सम्पूज्याग्रे निषीदन्तं दत्तात्रेयमुवाच तम् ॥ २०

मयोपहूतः सम्प्राप्तो दत्तात्रेय महामुने ।
स्मर्तृगामी त्वमित्येतत् किंवदन्ती परीक्षितुम् ॥ २१

मयाद्य संस्मृतोऽसि त्वमपराधं क्षमस्व मे ।
दत्तात्रेयो मुनिं प्राह मम प्रकृतिरीदृशी ॥ २२

अभक्त्या वा सुभक्त्या वा यः स्मरेन्मामनन्यधीः ।
तदानीं तमुपागत्य ददामि तदभीप्सितम् ॥ २३

दत्तात्रेयो मुनिं प्राह दलादनमुनीश्वरम् ।
यदिष्टं तद्वृणीष्व त्वं यत् प्राप्तोऽहं त्वया स्मृतः ॥ २४

दत्तात्रेयं मुनिः प्राह मया किमपि नोच्यते ।
त्वच्चित्ते यत्स्थितं तन्मे प्रयच्छ मुनिपुङ्गव ॥ २५

श्रीदत्तात्रेय उवाच ।

ममास्ति वज्रकवचं गृहाणेत्यवदन्मुनिम् ।
तथ्येत्यङ्गीकृतवते दलादनमुनये मुनिः ॥ २६

स्ववज्रकवचं प्राह ऋषिच्छन्दःपुरःसरम् ।
न्यासं ध्यानं फलं तत्र प्रयोजनमशेषतः ॥ २७

अस्य श्रीदत्तात्रेयवज्रकवचस्तोत्रमन्त्रस्य, किरातरूपी महारुद्र ऋषिः, अनुष्टुप् छन्दः,
श्रीदत्तात्रेयो देवता, द्रां बीजं, आं शक्तिः,
क्रौं कीलकं, ॐ आत्मने नमः । ॐ द्रीं मनसे नमः ।
ॐ आं द्रीं श्रीं सौः ॐ क्लां क्लीं क्लूं क्लैं क्लौं क्लः ।
श्रीदत्तात्रेयप्रसादसिद्ध्यर्थे जपे विनियोगः ॥

करन्यासः ।

ॐ द्रां अङ्गुष्ठाभ्यां नमः । ॐ द्रीं तर्जनीभ्यां नमः । ॐ द्रूं मध्यमाभ्यां नमः ।
ॐ द्रैं अनामिकाभ्यां नमः । ॐ द्रौं कनिष्ठिकाभ्यां नमः ।
ॐ द्रः करतलकरपृष्ठाभ्यां नमः ॥

हृदयादिन्यासः ।

ॐ द्रां हृदयाय नमः । ॐ द्रीं शिरसे स्वाहा । ॐ द्रूं शिखायै वषट् ।
ॐ द्रैं कवचाय हुं । ॐ द्रौं नेत्रत्रयाय वौषट् । ॐ द्रः अस्त्राय फट् ।
ॐ भूर्भुवःस्वरोमिति दिग्बन्धः ॥

ध्यानम् ।

जगदङ्कुरकन्दाय सच्चिदानन्दमूर्तये । दत्तात्रेयाय योगीन्द्रचन्द्राय परमात्मने ॥ १

कदा योगी कदा भोगी कदा नग्नः पिशाचवत् ।
दत्तात्रेयो हरिः साक्षाद्भुक्तिमुक्तिप्रदायकः ॥ २

वाराणसीपुरस्नायी कोल्हापुरजपादरः । माहुरीपुरभिक्षाशी सह्यशायी दिगम्बर ॥ ३
इन्द्रनीलसमाकारश्चन्द्रकान्तिसमद्युतिः । वैडुर्यसदृशस्फूर्तिश्चलत्किञ्चिज्जटाधरः ॥ ४

स्निग्धधावल्ययुक्ताक्षोऽत्यन्तनीलकनीनिकः ।
भ्रूवक्षःश्मश्रुनीलाङ्कः सशाङ्कसदृशाननः ॥ ५

हासनिर्जितनीहारः कण्ठनिर्जितकम्बुकः ।
मांसलांसो दीर्घबाहुः पाणिनिर्जितपल्लवः ॥ ६

विशालपीनवक्षाश्च ताम्रपाणिर्दलोदरः । पृथुलश्रोणिललितो विशालजघनस्थलः ॥ ७

रम्भास्तम्भोपमानोरुर्जानुपूर्वैकजङ्घकः । गूढगुल्फः कूर्मपृष्ठोलसत्पादोषरिस्थलः ॥८

रक्तारविन्दसदृशरमणीयपदाधरः । चर्माम्बरधरो योगी स्मर्तृगामी क्षणे क्षणे ॥ ९

ज्ञानोपदेशनीरतो विपद्धरणदीक्षितः । सिद्धासनसमासीन ऋजुकायो हसन्मुखः ॥ १०

वामहस्तेन वरदो दक्षिणेनाभयङ्करः ।
बालोन्मत्तपिशाचीभिः क्वचिद्युक्तः परीक्षितः ॥ ११

त्यागी भोगी महायोगी नित्यानन्दो निरञ्जनः ।
सर्वरूपी सर्वदाता सर्वगः सर्वकामदः ॥ १२

भस्मोद्धूलितसर्वाङ्गो महापातकनाशनः ।
भुक्तिप्रदो मुक्तिदाता जीवन्मुक्तो न संशयः ॥ १३

एवं ध्यात्वाऽनन्यचित्तो मद्वज्रकवचं पठेत् ।
मामेव पश्यन्सर्वत्र स मया सह सञ्चरेत् ॥ १४

दिगम्बरं भस्मसुगन्धलेपनं चक्रं त्रिशूलं डमरुं गदायुधम् ।
पद्मासनं योगिमुनीन्द्रवन्दितं दत्तेति नामस्मरणेन नित्यम् ॥ १५

(अथ पञ्चोपचारैः संपूज्य ॐ द्रां इति अष्टोत्तरशतवारं जपेत्)

Now after doing *Panca Puja* the *Moola Mantra* "ॐ द्रां" has to be chant 108 times.

ॐ द्राम् ।

कवचम् ।

ॐ दत्तात्रेयः शिरः पातु सहस्राब्जेषु संस्थितः ।
भालं पात्वानसूयेयश्चन्द्रमण्डलमध्यगः ॥ १

कूर्चं मनोमयः पातु हं क्षं द्विदलपद्मभूः ।
ज्योतिरूपोऽक्षिणी पातु पातु शब्दात्मकः श्रुती ॥ २

नासिकां पातु गन्धात्मा मुखं पातु रसात्मकः ।
जिह्वां वेदात्मकः पातु दन्तोष्ठौ पातु धार्मिकः ॥ ३

कपोलावत्रिभूः पातु पात्वशेषं ममात्ववित् ।
स्वरात्मा षोडशाराब्जस्थितः स्वात्माऽवताद्गलम् ॥ ४

स्कन्धौ चन्द्रानुजः पातु भुजौ पातु कृतादिभूः ।
जत्रुणी शत्रुजित् पातु पातु वक्षःस्थलं हरिः ॥ ५

कादिठान्तद्वादशारपद्मगो मरुदात्मकः । योगीश्वरेश्वरः पातु हृदयं हृदयस्थितः ॥ ६

पार्श्वे हरिः पार्श्ववर्ती पातु पार्श्वस्थितः स्मृतः ।

हठयोगादियोगज्ञः कुक्षी पातु कृपानिधिः ॥ ७

डकारादिफकारान्तदशारसरसीरुहे । नाभिस्थले वर्तमानो नाभिं वह्न्यात्मकोऽवतु ॥ ८

वह्नितत्वमयो योगी रक्षतान्मणिपूरकम् । कटिं कटिस्थब्रह्माण्डवासुदेवात्मकोऽवतु॥९

बकारादिलकारान्तषट्पत्राम्बुजबोधकः । (वक्रादि)
जलतत्वमयो योगी स्वाधिष्ठानं ममावतु ॥ १०

सिद्धासनसमासीन ऊरू सिद्धेश्वरोऽवतु । वादिसान्तचतुष्पत्रसरोरुहनिबोधकः ॥ ११

मूलाधारं महीरूपो रक्षताद्वीर्यनिग्रही । पृष्ठं च सर्वतः पातु जान्युन्यस्तकराम्बुजः ॥ १२

जङ्घे पात्ववधूतेन्द्रः पात्वङ्घ्री तीर्थपावनः ।
सर्वाङ्गं पातु सर्वात्मा रोमाण्यवतु केशवः ॥ १३

चर्म चर्माम्बरः पातु रक्तं भक्तिप्रियोऽवतु ।
मांसं मांसकरः पातु मज्जां मज्जात्मकोऽवतु ॥ १४

अस्थीनि स्थिरधीः पायान्मेधां वेधाः प्रपालयेत् ।
शुक्रं सुखकरः पातु चित्तं पातु दृढाकृतिः ॥ १५

मनोबुद्धिमहङ्कारं हृषीकेशात्मकोऽवतु ।
कर्मेन्द्रियाणि पात्वीशः पातु ज्ञानेन्द्रियाण्यजः ॥ १६

बन्धून् बन्धूत्तमः पायाच्छत्रुभ्यः पातु शत्रुजित् ।
गृहारामधनक्षेत्रपुत्रादीञ्छङ्करोऽवतु ॥ १७

भार्यां प्रकृतिवित् पातु पश्वादीन्पातु शार्ङ्गभृत् ।
प्राणान्पातु प्रधानज्ञो भक्ष्यादीन्पातु भास्करः ॥ १८

सुखं चन्द्रात्मकः पातु दुःखात् पातु पुरान्तकः ।
पशून्पशूपतिः पातु भूतिं भूतेश्वरो मम ॥ १९

प्राच्यां विषहरः पातु पात्वाग्नेय्यां मखात्मकः ।
याम्यां धर्मात्मकः पातु नैरृत्यां सर्ववैरिहृत् ॥ २०

वराहः पातु वारुण्यां वायव्यां प्राणदोऽवतु ।

कौबेर्यां धनदः पातु पात्वैशान्यां महागुरुः ॥ २१

उर्ध्वं पातु महासिद्धः पात्वधस्ताज्जटाधरः ।
रक्षाहीनं तु यत्स्थानं रक्षत्वादिमुनीश्वरः ॥ २२

ॐ द्राम् । मालामन्त्रजपः । (पुनः – again)

करन्यासः ।

ॐ द्रां अङ्गुष्ठाभ्यां नमः । ॐ द्रीं तर्जनीभ्यां नमः । ॐ द्रूं मध्यमाभ्यां नमः ।
ॐ द्रैं अनामिकाभ्यां नमः । ॐ द्रौं कनिष्ठिकाभ्यां नमः ।
ॐ द्रः करतलकरपृष्ठाभ्यां नमः ॥

हृदयादिन्यासः ।

ॐ द्रां हृदयाय नमः । ॐ द्रीं शिरसे स्वाहा । ॐ द्रूं शिखायै वषट् ।
ॐ द्रैं कवचाय हुं । ॐ द्रौं नेत्रत्रयाय वौषट् । ॐ द्रः अस्त्राय फट् ।
ॐ भूर्भुवःस्वरोमिति दिग्विमोगः ॥

एतन्मे वज्रकवचं यः पठेच्छृणुयादपि ।वज्रकायश्चिरञ्जीवी दत्तात्रेयोऽहमब्रुवम् ॥ २३

त्यागी भोगी महायोगी सुखदुःखविवर्जितः ।
सर्वत्रसिद्धसङ्कल्पो जीवन्मुक्तोऽद्य वर्तते ॥ २४

इत्युक्त्वान्तर्दधे योगी दत्तात्रेयो दिगम्बरः ।
दलादनोऽपि तज्जप्त्वा जीवन्मुक्तः स वर्तते ॥ २५

भिल्लो दूरश्रवा नाम तदानीं श्रुतवादिनम् ।
सकृच्छ्रवणमात्रेण वज्राङ्गोऽभवदप्यसौ ॥ २६

इत्येतद्वज्रकवचं दत्तात्रेयस्य योगिनः ।
श्रुत्वाशेषं शम्भुमुखात् पुनरप्याह पार्वती ॥ २७

पार्वत्युवाच ।

एतत्कवचमाहात्म्यं वद विस्तरतो मम ।
कुत्र केन कदा जाप्यं किं यजाप्यं कथं कथम् ॥ २८

उवाच शम्भुस्तत्सर्वं पार्वत्या विनयोदितम् ।

श्री शिव उवाच ।

श्रुणु पार्वति वक्ष्यामि समाहितमनाविलम् ॥ २९

धर्मार्थकाममोक्षाणामिदमेव परायणम् । हस्त्यश्वरथपादातिसर्वैश्वर्यप्रदायकम् ॥ ३०

पुत्रमित्रकलत्रादिसर्वसन्तोषसाधनम् । वेदशास्त्रादिविद्यानां निधानं परमं हि तत् ॥ ३१

सङ्गीतशास्त्रसाहित्यसत्कवित्वविधायकम् ।
बुद्धिविद्यास्मृतिप्रज्ञामतिप्रौढिप्रदायकम् ॥ ३२

सर्वसन्तोषकरणं सर्वदुःखनिवारणम् । शत्रु संहारकं शीघ्रं यशःकीर्तिविवर्धनम् ॥ ३३

अष्टसंख्या महारोगाः सन्निपातास्त्रयोदश ।
षण्णवत्यक्षिरोगाश्च विंशतिर्मेहरोगकाः ॥ ३४

अष्टादश तु कुष्ठानि गुल्मान्यष्टविधान्यपि ।
अशीतिर्वातरोगाश्च चत्वारिशत्तु पैत्तिकाः ॥ ३५

विंशतिश्लेष्मरोगाश्च क्षयचातुर्थिकादयः ।
मन्त्रयन्त्रकुयोगाद्याः कल्पतन्त्रादिनिर्मिताः ॥ ३६

ब्रह्मराक्षसवेतालकूष्माण्डादिग्रहोद्भवाः ।
सङ्गजाः देशकालस्थास्तापत्रयसमुत्थिताः ॥ ३७

नवग्रहसमुद्भूता महापातकसम्भवाः ।सर्वे रोगाः प्रणश्यन्ति सहस्रावर्तनाद्ध्रुवम् ॥३८

अयुतावृत्तिमात्रेण वन्ध्या पुत्रवती भवेत् ।
अयुतद्वितयावृत्त्या ह्यपमृत्युजयो भवेत् ॥ ३९

अयुतत्रितयाच्चैव खेचरत्वं प्रजायते ।
सहस्रादयुतादर्वाक् सर्वकार्याणि साधयेत् ॥ ४०

लक्षावृत्या कार्यसिद्धिर्भवेत्येव न संशयः ॥ ४१

विषवृक्षस्य मूलेषु तिष्ठन् वै दक्षिणामुखः ।
कुरुते मासमात्रेण वैरिणं विकलेन्द्रियम् ॥ ४२

औदुम्बरतरोर्मूले वृद्धिकामेन जाप्यते ।
श्रीवक्षमूले श्रीकामी तिन्तिणी शान्तिकर्मणि ॥ ४३

ओजस्कामोऽश्वत्थमूले स्त्रीकामैः सहकारके ।
ज्ञानार्थी तुलसीमूले गर्भगेहे सुतार्थिभिः ॥ ४४

धनार्थिभिस्तु सुक्षेत्रे पशुकामैस्तु गोष्ठके ।
देवालये सर्वकामैस्तत्काले सर्वदर्शितम् ॥ ४५

नाभिमात्रजले स्थित्वा भानुमालोक्य यो जपेत् ।
युद्धे वा शास्त्रवादे वा सहस्रेण जयो भवेत् ॥ ४६

कण्ठमात्रे जले स्थित्वा यो रात्रौ कवचं पठेत् ।
ज्वरापस्मारकुष्ठादितापज्वरनिवारणम् ॥ ४७

यत्र यत्स्यात्स्थिरं यद्यत्प्रसन्नं तन्निवर्तते ।
तेन तत्र हि जप्तव्यं ततः सिद्धिर्भवेद्ध्रुवम् ॥ ४८

इत्युक्त्वान् च शिवो गौर्ये रहस्यं परमं शुभम् ।
यः पठेत् वज्रकवचं दत्तात्रेयोसमो भवेत् ॥ ४९

एवं शिवेन कथितं हिमवत्सुतायैप्रोक्तं दलादमुनयेऽत्रिसुतेनपूर्वम् ।
यः कोऽपि वज्रकवचं पठतीह लोके दत्तोपमश्चरति योगिवरश्चिरायुः ॥ ५०

इति श्री रुद्रयामले हिमवत्खण्डे मन्त्र शास्त्रे उपासना खण्डे शिव विजय सिद्धान्ते उमा महेश्वर संवादे श्री दत्तात्रेय वज्र कवच स्तोत्रं सम्पूर्णम् ॥

श्री दत्तात्रेयार्पणमस्तु ।

*****

Śrī Dattātreya Aṣṭottara Śata Nāmāvalī

108 divine names on *Śrī Dattātreya Bhagawan.*

Śrī Dattātreya Dhyānam

Dattātreyaṃ Śivaṃ Śāntaṃ Saccidānandamadvayam |
Ātmarūpaṃ Paraṃ Divyamavaṇyamupāsmahe || 1

Dattātreyaṃ Śivaṃ Śāntamindranīlanibhaṃ Prabhum |
Ātmamāyārataṃ Devaṃ Avadhūtaṃ Digambaram || 2

Bhasmoddhūlitasarvāṅgaṃ Jaṭājūṭadharaṃ Vibhum |
Caturbāhumudārāṅgaṃ Praphullakamalekṣaṇam || 3

Jñānayoganidhiṃ Viśvaguruṃ Yogijanapriyam |
Bhaktānukampanaṃ Sarvasākṣiṇaṃ Siddhasevitam || 4

Jaṭādharaṃ Pāṇḍuraṅgaṃ Śūlahastaṃ Kṛpānidhim |
(Pāṇḍurāṅgaṃ)
Sarvarogaharaṃ Devaṃ Dattātreyamahaṃ Bhaje || 5

Mālā Kamaṇḍaluradhaḥ Karapadmayugme
Madhyasthapāṇiyugale Ḍamarutriśūle |
Yannyasta Ūrdhvakarayoḥ Śubhaśaṅkhacakre
Vande Tamatrivaradaṃ Bhujaṣaṭka Yuktam || 6

Iti Śrī Dattātreya Dhyānaṃ Sampūrṇam |

श्री दत्तात्रेय ध्यानम्

दत्तात्रेयं शिवं शान्तं सच्चिदानन्दमद्वयम् ।आत्मरूपं परं दिव्यमवण्यमुपास्महे ॥ १

दत्तात्रेयं शिवं शान्तमिन्द्रनीलनिभं प्रभुम् ।आत्ममायारतं देवं अवधूतं दिगम्बरम् ॥ २

भस्मोद्धूलितसर्वाङ्गं जटाजूटधरं विभुम् ।चतुर्बाहुमुदाराङ्गं प्रफुल्लकमलेक्षणम् ॥ ३

ज्ञानयोगनिधिं विश्वगुरुं योगिजनप्रियम् ।भक्तानुकम्पनं सर्वसाक्षिणं सिद्धसेवितम् ॥ ४

जटाधरं पाण्डुरङ्गं शूलहस्तं कृपानिधिम् । (पाण्डुराङ्गं)
सर्वरोगहरं देवं दत्तात्रेयमहं भजे ॥ ५॥

माला कमण्डलुरधः करपद्मयुग्मेमध्यस्थपाणियुगले डमरुत्रिशूले ।
यन्यस्त ऊर्ध्वकरयोः शुभशङ्खचक्रे वन्दे तमत्रिवरदं भुजषट्क युक्तम् ॥ ६॥

इति श्रीदत्तात्रेयध्यानं सम्पूर्णम् ।

Śrī Dattātreya Aṣṭottara Śata Nāmāvalī
श्री दत्तात्रेय अष्टोत्तर शत नामावली

1.	*Oṃ Śrīdattāya Namaḥ* |	ॐ श्रीदत्ताय नमः ।
2.	*Oṃ Devadattāya Namaḥ* |	ॐ देवदत्ताय नमः ।
3.	*Oṃ Brahmadattāya Namaḥ* |	ॐ ब्रह्मदत्ताय नमः ।
4.	*Oṃ Viṣṇudattāya Namaḥ* |	ॐ विष्णुदत्ताय नमः ।
5.	*Oṃ Śivadattāya Namaḥ* |	ॐ शिवदत्ताय नमः ।
6.	*Oṃ Atridattāya Namaḥ* |	ॐ अत्रिदत्ताय नमः ।
7.	*Oṃ Ātreyāya Namaḥ* |	ॐ आत्रेयाय नमः ।
8.	*Oṃ Atrivaradāya Namaḥ* |	ॐ अत्रिवरदाय नमः ।
9.	*Oṃ Anusūyāya Namaḥ* |	ॐ अनुसूयाय नमः ।
10.	*Oṃ Anasūyāsūnave Namaḥ* |	ॐ अनसूयासूनवे नमः ।
11.	*Oṃ Avadhūtāya Namaḥ* |	ॐ अवधूताय नमः ।
12.	*Oṃ Dharmāya Namaḥ* |	ॐ धर्माय नमः ।
13.	*Oṃ Dharmaparāyaṇāya Namaḥ*|	ॐ धर्मपरायणाय नमः ।
14.	*Oṃ Dharmapataye Namaḥ* |	ॐ धर्मपतये नमः ।
15.	*Oṃ Siddhāya Namaḥ* |	ॐ सिद्धाय नमः ।
16.	*Oṃ Siddhidāya Namaḥ* |	ॐ सिद्धिदाय नमः ।
17.	*Oṃ Siddhipataye Namaḥ* |	ॐ सिद्धिपतये नमः ।
18.	*Oṃ Siddhasevitāya Namaḥ* |	ॐ सिद्धसेविताय नमः ।
19.	*Oṃ Gurave Namaḥ* |	ॐ गुरवे नमः ।
20.	*Oṃ Gurugamyāya Namaḥ* |	ॐ गुरुगम्याय नमः ।
21.	*Oṃ Gurorgurutarāya Namaḥ* |	ॐ गुरोर्गुरुतराय नमः ।
22.	*Oṃ Gariṣṭhāya Namaḥ* |	ॐ गरिष्ठाय नमः ।

23.	*Oṃ Variṣṭhāya Namaḥ* |	ॐ वरिष्ठाय नमः।
24.	*Oṃ Mahiṣṭhāya Namaḥ* |	ॐ महिष्ठाय नमः।
25.	*Oṃ Mahātmane Namaḥ* |	ॐ महात्मने नमः।
26.	*Oṃ Yogāya Namaḥ* |	ॐ योगाय नमः।
27.	*Oṃ Yogagamyāya Namaḥ* |	ॐ योगगम्याय नमः।
28.	*Oṃ Yogīdeśakarāya Namaḥ* |	ॐ योगीदेशकराय नमः।
29.	*Oṃ Yogarataye Namaḥ* |	ॐ योगरतये नमः।
30.	*Oṃ Yogīśāya Namaḥ* |	ॐ योगीशाय नमः।
31.	*Oṃ Yogādhīśāya Namaḥ* |	ॐ योगाधीशाय नमः।
32.	*Oṃ Yogaparāyaṇāya Namaḥ* |	ॐ योगपरायणाय नमः।
33.	*Oṃ Yogidhyeyāṅghripaṅkajāya Namaḥ* |	ॐ योगिध्येयाङ्घ्रि पङ्कजाय नमः।
34.	*Oṃ Digambarāya Namaḥ* |	ॐ दिगम्बराय नमः।
35.	*Oṃ Divyāmbarāya Namaḥ* |	ॐ दिव्याम्बराय नमः।
36.	*Oṃ Pītāmbarāya Namaḥ* |	ॐ पीताम्बराय नमः।
37.	*Oṃ Śvetāmbarāya Namaḥ* |	ॐ श्वेताम्बराय नमः।
38.	*Oṃ Citrāmbarāya Namaḥ* |	ॐ चित्राम्बराय नमः।
39.	*Oṃ Bālāya Namaḥ* |	ॐ बालाय नमः।
40.	*Oṃ Bālavīryāya Namaḥ* |	ॐ बालवीर्याय नमः।
41.	*Oṃ Kumārāya Namaḥ* |	ॐ कुमाराय नमः।
42.	*Oṃ Kiśorāya Namaḥ* |	ॐ किशोराय नमः।
43.	*Oṃ Kandarpamohanāya Namaḥ*	ॐ कन्दर्पमोहनाय नमः।
44.	*Oṃ Ardhāṅgāliṅgitāṅganāya Namaḥ* |	ॐ अर्धाङ्गा लिङ्गि ताङ्गनाय नमः।
45.	*Oṃ Surāgāya Namaḥ* |	ॐ सुरागाय नमः।
46.	*Oṃ Virāgāya Namaḥ* |	ॐ विरागाय नमः।
47.	*Oṃ Vītarāgāya Namaḥ* |	ॐ वीतरागाय नमः।
48.	*Oṃ Amṛtavarṣiṇe Namaḥ* |	ॐ अमृतवर्षिणे नमः।
49.	*Oṃ Ugrāya Namaḥ* |	ॐ उग्राय नमः।
50.	*Oṃ Anugrarūpāya Namaḥ* |	ॐ अनुग्ररूपाय नमः।
51.	*Oṃ Sthavirāya Namaḥ* |	ॐ स्थविराय नमः।
52.	*Oṃ Sthavīyase Namaḥ* |	ॐ स्थवीयसे नमः।
53.	*Oṃ Śāntāya Namaḥ* |	ॐ शान्ताय नमः।

54.	*Oṃ Aghorāya Namaḥ* |	ॐ अघोराय नमः ।
55.	*Oṃ Gūḍhāya Namaḥ* |	ॐ गूढाय नमः ।
56.	*Oṃ Ūrdhvaretase Namaḥ* |	ॐ ऊर्ध्वरेतसे नमः ।
57.	*Oṃ Ekavaktrāya Namaḥ* |	ॐ एकवक्त्राय नमः ।
58.	*Oṃ Anekavaktrāya Namaḥ* |	ॐ अनेकवक्त्राय नमः ।
59.	*Oṃ Dvinetrāya Namaḥ* |	ॐ द्विनेत्राय नमः ।
60.	*Oṃ Trinetrāya Namaḥ* |	ॐ त्रिनेत्राय नमः ।
61.	*Oṃ Dvibhujāya Namaḥ* |	ॐ द्विभुजाय नमः ।
62.	*Oṃ Ṣaḍbhujāya Namaḥ* |	ॐ षड्भुजाय नमः ।
63.	*Oṃ Akṣamāline Namaḥ* |	ॐ अक्षमालिने नमः ।
64.	*Oṃ Kamaṇḍaludhāriṇe Namaḥ* |	ॐ कमण्डलुधारिणे नमः।
65.	*Oṃ Śūline Namaḥ* |	ॐ शूलिने नमः ।
66.	*Oṃ Ḍamarudhāriṇe Namaḥ* |	ॐ डमरुधारिणे नमः ।
67.	*Oṃ Śaṅkhine Namaḥ* |	ॐ शङ्खिने नमः ।
68.	*Oṃ Gadine Namaḥ* |	ॐ गदिने नमः ।
69.	*Oṃ Munaye Namaḥ* |	ॐ मुनये नमः ।
70.	*Oṃ Mauline Namaḥ* |	ॐ मौलिने नमः ।
71.	*Oṃ Virūpāya Namaḥ* |	ॐ विरूपाय नमः ।
72.	*Oṃ Svarūpāya Namaḥ* |	ॐ स्वरूपाय नमः ।
73.	*Oṃ Sahasraśirase Namaḥ* |	ॐ सहस्रशिरसे नमः ।
74.	*Oṃ Sahasrākṣāya Namaḥ* |	ॐ सहस्राक्षाय नमः ।
75.	*Oṃ Sahasrabāhave Namaḥ* |	ॐ सहस्रबाहवे नमः ।
76.	*Oṃ Sahasrāyudhāya Namaḥ* |	ॐ सहस्रायुधाय नमः ।
77.	*Oṃ Sahasrapādāya Namaḥ* |	ॐ सहस्रपादाय नमः ।
78.	*Oṃ Sahasrapadmārcitāya Namaḥ* |	ॐ सहस्रपद्मार्चिताय नमः ।
79.	*Oṃ Padmahastāya Namaḥ* |	ॐ पद्महस्ताय नमः ।
80.	*Oṃ Padmapādāya Namaḥ* |	ॐ पद्मपादाय नमः ।
81.	*Oṃ Padmanābhāya Namaḥ* |	ॐ पद्मनाभाय नमः ।
82.	*Oṃ Padmamāline Namaḥ* |	ॐ पद्ममालिने नमः ।
83.	*Oṃ Padmagarbhāruṇākṣāya Namaḥ* |	ॐ पद्मगर्भारुणाक्षाय नमः ।

84.	*Oṃ Padmakiñjalkavarcase Namaḥ |*	ॐ पद्मकिञ्जल्कवर्चसे नमः ।
85.	*Oṃ Jñānine Namaḥ |*	ॐ ज्ञानिने नमः ।
86.	*Oṃ Jñānagamyāya Namaḥ |*	ॐ ज्ञानगम्याय नमः ।
87.	*Oṃ Jñānavijñānamūrtaye Namaḥ |*	ॐ ज्ञानविज्ञानमूर्तये नमः ।
88.	*Oṃ Dhyānine Namaḥ |*	ॐ ध्यानिने नमः ।
89.	*Oṃ Dhyānaniṣṭhāya Namaḥ |*	ॐ ध्याननिष्ठाय नमः ।
90.	*Oṃ Dhyānastimitamūrtaye Namaḥ |*	ॐ ध्यानस्तिमितमूर्तये नमः ।
91.	*Oṃ Dhūlidhūsaritāṅgāya Namaḥ* ।	ॐ धूलिधूसरिताङ्गाय नमः ।
92.	*Oṃ Candanaliptamūrtaye Namaḥ |*	ॐ चन्दनलिप्तमूर्तये नमः ।
93.	*Oṃ Bhasmoddhūlitadehāya Namaḥ |*	ॐ भस्मोद्धूलितदेहाय नमः ।
94.	*Oṃ Divyagandhānulepine Namaḥ |*	ॐ दिव्यगन्धानुलेपिने नमः ।
95.	*Oṃ Prasannāya Namaḥ |*	ॐ प्रसन्नाय नमः ।
96.	*Oṃ Pramattāya Namaḥ |*	ॐ प्रमत्ताय नमः ।
97.	*Oṃ Prakṛṣṭārthapradāya Namaḥ*	ॐ प्रकृष्टार्थप्रदाय नमः ।
98.	*Oṃ Aṣṭaiśvaryapradāya Namaḥ|*	ॐ अष्टैश्वर्यप्रदाय नमः ।
99.	*Oṃ Varadāya Namaḥ |*	ॐ वरदाय नमः ।
100.	*Oṃ Varīyase Namaḥ |*	ॐ वरीयसे नमः ।
101.	*Oṃ Brahmaṇe Namaḥ |*	ॐ ब्रह्मणे नमः ।
102.	*Oṃ Brahmarūpāya Namaḥ |*	ॐ ब्रह्मरूपाय नमः ।
103.	*Oṃ Viṣṇave Namaḥ |*	ॐ विष्णवे नमः ।
104.	*Oṃ Viśvarūpiṇe Namaḥ |*	ॐ विश्वरूपिणे नमः ।
105.	*Oṃ Śaṅkarāya Namaḥ |*	ॐ शङ्कराय नमः ।

106.	*Oṃ Ātmane Namaḥ* |	ॐ आत्मने नमः ।
107.	*Oṃ Antarātmane Namaḥ* |	ॐ अन्तरात्मने नमः ।
108.	*Oṃ Paramātmane Namaḥ* |	ॐ परमात्मने नमः ।

*****

Śrīmad Dattātreya Sahasranāma Stotram

This Sahasranama Stotram on *Śrīmad Dattātreya* is from Brahmanda Puranam, as a dialogue between Sage Naradar and Sages Sanat Kumaras. One Thousand divine names on *Śrīmad Dattātreya* have been culminated from 142 shlokas of this Stotram, which are given in the next chapter.

There is one other version of Sahasranama on *Śrī Dattātreya* written by *Śrī Parama Pūjya Paramahaṃsa Parivrājakācārya Śrī Śrī Śrīmad Vāsudevānanda Sarasvatī Yati Vareṇya* Swamijee. The beauty of this Sahasranama, is that all the 1,000 names start only with the letter *'Da'* and its family. Hence, it is called as *Dakārādi Datta Sahasranāmam.* Since the Sahasranama given below is an older one and also from a Purana, it has been followed by most and we also.

Stotram

Nikhilāgamatattvajña Brahmajñānaparāyaṇa I
Vadāsmākaṃ Muktyupāyaṃ Sūta Sarvopakārakam II 1

Sarvadeveṣu Ko Devaḥ Sadyo Mokṣaprado Bhavet I
Ko Manurvā Bhavettasya Sadyaḥ Prītikaro Dhruvam II 2

Sūta Uvāca –

Nigamāgamatattvajño Hyavadhūtaścidambaraḥ I
Bhaktavātsalyapravaṇo Datta Eva Hi Kevalaḥ II 3

Sadā Prasannavadano Bhaktacintaikatatparaḥ I
Tasya Nāmānyanantāni Vartante'thāpyadaḥ Param II 4

Dattasya Nāmasāhasraṃ Tasya Prītivivardhanam I
Yastvidaṃ Paṭhate Nityaṃ Dattātreyaikamānasaḥ II 5

Mucyate Sarvapāpebhyaḥ Sa Sasdyo Nātra Saṃśayaḥ I
Ante Taddhāma Saṃyāti Punarāvṛttidurlabham II 6

Nyāsam

Asya Śrīmad Dattātreya Sahasranāma Stotra Mantrasya

Avadhūta Ṛṣiḥ I Anuṣṭupchandaḥ I Digambaro Devatā I

Oṃ Bījam I Hrīṃ Śaktiḥ I Krauṃ Kīlakam I

Śrī Dattātreya Prītyarthe Jape Viniyogaḥ II

Dhyānam

Digambaraṃ Bhasmavilepitāṅgaṃ Bodhātmakaṃ Muktikaraṃ Prasannam I

Nirmānasaṃ Śyāmatanuṃ Bhaje'haṃ Dattātreyaṃ Brahma Samādhiyuktam II

Sahasra Nāma Stotram I

Dattātreyo Mahoyogī Yogeśaścāmaraprabhum I
Munirdigambaro Bālo Māyāmukto Madāpahaḥ II 1

Avadhūto Mahānāthaḥ Śaṅkaro'maravallabhaḥ I
Mahādevaścādidevaḥ Purāṇaprabhurīśvaraḥ II 2

Sattvakṛtsattvabhṛdbhāvaḥ Sattvātmā Sattvasāgaraḥ I
Sattvavitsattvasākṣī Ca Sattvasādhyo'marādhipaḥ II 3

Bhūtakṛdbhūtabhṛccaiva Bhūtātmā Bhūtasambhavaḥ I
Bhūtabhāvo Bhavo Bhūtavittathā Bhūtakāraṇaḥ II 4

Bhūtasākṣī Prabhūtiśca Bhūtānāṃ Paramā Gatiḥ I
Bhūtasaṅgavihīnātmā Bhūtātmā Bhūtaśaṅkaraḥ II 5

Bhūtanātho Mahānāthaścādinātho Maheśvaraḥ I
Sarvabhūtanivāsātmā Bhūtasantāpanāśanaḥ II 6

Sarvātmā Sarvabhṛtsarvaḥ Sarvajñaḥ Sarvanirṇayaḥ I
Sarvasākṣī Bṛhadbhānuḥ Sarvavitsarvamaṅgalaḥ II 7

Śāntaḥ Satyaḥ Samaḥ Pūrṇo Hyekākī Kamalāpatiḥ I

Rāmo Rāmapriyaścaiva Virāmo Rāmakāraṇam I I 8

Śuddhātmā Pāvano'nantaḥ Pratītaḥ Paramārthabhṛt I

Haṃsasākṣī Vibhuścaiva Prabhuḥ Pralaya Ityapi I I 9

Siddhātmā Paramātmā Ca Siddhānāṃ Paramā Gatiḥ I

Siddhisiddhastathā Sādhyaḥ Sādhano Hyuttamastathā I I 10

Sulakṣaṇaḥ Sumedhāvī Vidyāvānvigatāntaraḥ I

Vijvaraśca Mahābāhurbahulānandavardhanaḥ I I 11

Avyaktapuruṣaḥ Prājñaḥ Parajñaḥ Paramārthadṛk I

Parāparavinirmukto Yuktastattvaprakāśavān I I 12

Dayāvānbhagavānbhāvī Bhāvātmā Bhāvakāraṇaḥ I

Bhavasantāpanāśaśca Puṣpavānpaṇḍito Budhaḥ I I 13

Pratyakṣavasturviśvātmā Pratyagbrahma Sanātanaḥ I

Pramāṇavigataścaiva Pratyāhāraniyojakaḥ I I 14

Praṇavaḥ Praṇavātītaḥ Pramukhaḥ Pralayātmakaḥ I

Mṛtyuñjayo Viviktātmā Śaṅkarātmā Paro Vapuḥ I I 15

Paramastanuvijñeyaḥ Paramātmani Saṃsthitaḥ I

Prabodhakalanādhāraḥ Prabhāvapravarottamaḥ I I 16

Cidambaraścidvilāsaścidākāśaściduttamaḥ I

Cittacaitanyacittātmā Devānāṃ Paramā Gatiḥ I I 17

Acetyaścetanādhāraścetanācittavikramaḥ I

Cittātmā Cetanārūpo Lasatpaṅkajalocanaḥ I I 18

Parabrahma Paraṃ Jyotiḥ Paraṃ Dhāma Parantapaḥ I

Paraṃ Sūtraṃ Paraṃ Tantraṃ Pavitraṃ Paramohavān I I 19

Kṣetrajñaḥ Kṣetragaḥ Kṣetraḥ Kṣetrādhāraḥ Purañjanaḥ I
Kṣetraśūnyo Lokasākṣī Kṣetravānbahunāyakaḥ I I 20

Yogendo Yogapūjyaśca Yoga Ātmavidāṃ Śuciḥ I
Yogamāyādharaḥ Sthāṇuracalaḥ Kamalāpatiḥ I I 21

Yogeśo Yoganirmātā Yogajñānaprakāśanaḥ I
Yogapālo Lokapālaḥ Saṃsāratamanāśanaḥ I I 22

Guhyo Guhyatamo Gupto Mukto Yuktaḥ Sanātanaḥ I
Gahano Gaganākāro Gambhīro Gaṇanāyakaḥ I I 23

Govindo Gopatirgoptā Gobhāgo Bhāvasaṃsthitaḥ I
Gosākṣī Gotamāriśca Gāndhāro Gaganākṛtiḥ I I 24

Yogayukto Bhogayuktaḥ Śaṅkāmuktasamādhimān I
Sahajaḥ Sakaleśānaḥ Kārtavīryavarapradaḥ I I 25

Sarajā Virajāḥ Puṃso Pāvanaḥ Pāpanāśanaḥ I *Pumān*
Parāvaravinirmuktaḥ Parañjyotiḥ Purātanaḥ I I 26

Nānājyotiranekātmā Svayañjyotiḥ Sadāśivaḥ I
Divyajyotirmayaścaiva Satyavijñānabhāskaraḥ I I 27

Nityaśuddhaḥ Paraḥ Pūrṇaḥ Prakāśaḥ Prakaṭodbhavaḥ I
Pramādavigataścaiva Pareśaḥ Paravikramaḥ I I 28

Yogī Yogo Yogapaśca Yogābhyāsaprakāśanaḥ I
Yoktā Moktā Vidhātā Ca Trātā Pātā Nirāyudhyaḥ I I 29

Nityamukto Nityayuktaḥ Satyaḥ Satyaparākramaḥ I
Sattvaśuddhikaraḥ Sattvastathā Sattvambhṛtāṃ Gatiḥ I I 30

Śrīdharaḥ Śrīvapuḥ Śrīmān Śrīnivāso'marārcitaḥ I
Śrīnidhiḥ Śrīpatiḥ Śreṣṭhaḥ Śreyaskaścaramāśrayaḥ II 31

Tyāgī Tyāgārthasampannastyāgātmā Tyāgavigrahaḥ I
Tyāgalakṣaṇasiddhātmā Tyāgajñastyāgakāraṇaḥ II 32

Bhogo Bhoktā Tathā Bhogyo Bhogasādhanakāraṇaḥ I
Bhogī Bhogārthasampanno Bhogajñānaprakāśanaḥ II 33

Kevalaḥ Keśavaḥ Kṛṣṇaḥ Kaṃvāsāḥ Kamalālayaḥ I
Kamalāsanapūjyaśca Harirajñānakhaṇḍanaḥ II 34
Mahātmā Mahadādiśca Maheśottamavanditaḥ I
Manobuddhivihīnātmā Mānātmā Mānavādhipaḥ II 35

Bhuvaneśo Vibhūtiśca Dhṛtirmedhā Smṛtirdayā I
Duḥkhadāvānalo Buddhaḥ Prabuddhaḥ Parameśvaraḥ II 36

Kāmahā Krodhahā Caiva Dambhadarpamadāpahaḥ I
Ajñānapatimirāriśca Bhavārirbhuvaneśvaraḥ II 37

Rūpakudrūpabhṛdrūpī Rūpātmā Rūpakāraṇaḥ I
Rūpajño Rūpasākṣī Ca Nāmarūpo Guṇāntakaḥ II 38

Aprameyaḥ Prameyaśca Pramāṇaṃ Praṇavāśrayaḥ I
Pramāṇarahito'cintyaścetanāvigato'jaraḥ II 39

Akṣaro'kṣaramuktaśca Vijvaro Jvaranāśanaḥ I
Viśiṣṭo Vittaśāstrī Ca Dṛṣṭo Dṛṣṭāntavarjitaḥ II 40

Guṇeśo Guṇakāyaśca Guṇātmā Gaṇabhāvanaḥ I
Anantaguṇasampanno Guṇagarbho Guṇādhipaḥ II 41

Gaṇeśo Guṇanāthaśca Guṇātmā Gaṇabhāvanaḥ I
Gaṇabandhurvivekātmā Guṇayuktaḥ Parākramī II 42

Atarkyaḥ Kraturagniśca Kṛtajñaḥ Saphalāśrayaḥ I
Yajñaśca Yajñaphaldo Yajña Ijyo'marottamaḥ II 43

Hiraṇyagarbhaḥ Śrīgarbhaḥ Khagarbhaḥ Kuṇapeśvaraḥ I
Māyāgarbho Lokagarbhaḥ Svayambhūrbhuvanāntakaḥ II 44

Niṣpāpo Nibiḍo Nandī Bodhī Bodhasamāśrayaḥ I
Bodhātmā Bodhanātmā Ca Bhedavaitaṇḍakhaṇḍanaḥ II 45

Svābhāvyo Bhāvanirmukto Vyakto'vyaktasamāśrayaḥ I
Nityatṛpto Nirābhāso Nirvāṇaḥ Śaraṇaḥ Suhṛt II 46

Guhyeśo Guṇagambhīro Guṇadoṣanivāraṇaḥ I
Guṇasaṅgavihīnaśca Yogārerdarpanāśanaḥ II 47

Ānandaḥ Paramānandaḥ Svānandasukhavardhanaḥ I
Satyānandaścidānandaḥ Sarvānandaparāyaṇaḥ II 48

Sadrūpaḥ Sahajaḥ Satyaḥ Svānandaḥ Sumanoharaḥ I
Sarvaḥ Sarvāntaraścaiva Pūrvātpūrvatarastathā II 49

Khamayaḥ Khaparaḥ Khādiḥ Khambrahma Khatanuḥ Khagaḥ I
Khavāsāḥ Khavihīnaśca Khanidhiḥ Khaparāśrayaḥ II 50

Anantaścādirūpaśca Sūryamaṇḍalamadhyagaḥ I
Amoghaḥ Paramāmoghaḥ Parokṣaḥ Varadaḥ Kaviḥ II 51

Viśvacakṣurviśvasākṣī Viśvabāhurdhaneśvaraḥ I
Dhanañjayo Mahātejāstejiṣṭhastaijasaḥ Sukhī II 52

Jyotirjyotirmayo Jetā Jyotiṣāṃ Jyotirātmakaḥ I
Jyotiṣāmapi Jyotiśca Janako Janamohanaḥ II 53

Jitendriyo Jitakrodho Jitātmā Jitamānasaḥ I
Jitasaṅgo Jitaprāṇo Jitasaṃsāravāsanaḥ II 54

Nirvāsano Nirālambo Niryogakṣemavarjitaḥ I
Nirīho Nirahaṅkāro Nirāśīrnirupādhikaḥ I I 55

Nityabodho Viviktātmā Viśuddhottamagauravaḥ I
Vidyārthī Paramārthī Ca Śraddhārthī Sādhanātmakaḥ I I 56

Pratyāhārī Nirāhārī Sarvāhāraparāyaṇaḥ I
Nityaśuddho Nirākāṅkṣī Pārāyaṇaparāyaṇaḥ I I 57

Aṇoraṇutaraḥ Sūkṣmaḥ Sthūlaḥ Sthūlatarastathā I
Ekastathā'nekarūpo Viśvarūpaḥ Sanātanaḥ I I 58

Naikarūpo Virūpātmā Naikabodhamayo'pi Ca I
Naikanāmamayaścaiva Naikavidyāvivardhanaḥ I I 59

Ekaścaikāntikaścaiva Nānābhāvavivarjitaḥ I
Ekākṣarastathā Bījaḥ Pūrṇabimbaḥ Sanātanaḥ I I 60

Mantravīryo Mantrabījaḥ Śāstravīryo Jagatpatiḥ I
Nānāvīryadharaścaiva Śakreśaḥ Pṛthivīpatiḥ I I 61

Prāṇeśaḥ Prāṇadaḥ Prāṇaḥ Prāṇāyāmaparāyaṇaḥ I
Prāṇapañcakanirmuktaḥ Kośapañcakavarjitaḥ I I 62

Niścalo Niṣkalo'saṅgo Niṣprapañco Nirāmayaḥ I
Nirādhāro Nirākāro Nirvikāro Nirañjanaḥ I I 63

Niṣpratīto Nirābhāso Nirāsakto Nirākulaḥ I
Niṣṭhāsarvagataścaiva Nirārambho Nirāśrayaḥ I I 64

Nirantaraḥ Sattvagoptā Śānto Dānto Mahāmuniḥ I
Niḥśabdaḥ Sukṛtaḥ Svasthaḥ Satyavādī Sureśvaraḥ I I 65

Jñānado Jñānavijñānī Jñānātmā''nandapūritaḥ I
Jñānayajñavidāṃ Dakṣo Jñānāgnirjvalano Budhaḥ I I 66

Dayāvānbhavarogāriścikitsācaramāgatiḥ ।
Candramaṇḍalamadhyasthaścandrakoṭisuśītalaḥ ।। 67

Yantakṛtparamo Yantrī Yantrārūḍhaparājitaḥ ।
Yantravidyantravāsaśca Yantrādhāro Dharādharaḥ ।। 68

Tattvajñastattvabhūtātmā Mahattattvaprakāśanaḥ ।
Tattvasaṅkhyānayogajñaḥ Sāṅkhyaśāstrapravartakaḥ ।। 69

Anantavikramo Devo Mādhavaśca Dhaneśvaraḥ ।
Sādhuḥ Sādhuvariṣṭhātmā Sāvadhāno'marottamaḥ ।। 70

Niḥsaṅkalpo Nirādhāro Durdharo Hyātmavitpatiḥ ।
Ārogyasukhadaścaiva Pravaro Vāsavastathā ।। 71

Pareśaḥ Paramodāraḥ Pratyakcaitanyadurgamaḥ ।
Durādharṣo Durāvāso Dūratvaparināśanaḥ ।। 72

Vedavidvedakṛdvedo Vedātmā Vimalāśayaḥ ।
Viviktasevī Ca Saṃsāraśramanāśanastathā ।। 73

Brahmayonirbṛhadyonirviśvayonirvidehavān ।
Viśālākṣo Viśvanātho Hāṭakāṅgadabhūṣaṇaḥ ।। 74

Abādhyo Jagadārādhyo Jagadārjavapālanaḥ ।
Janavāndhanavāndharmī Dharmago Dharmavardhanaḥ ।। 75

Amṛtaḥ Śāśvataḥ Sādyaḥ Siddhidaḥ Sumanoharaḥ ।
Khalubrahmakhalusthāno Munīnāṃ Paramā Gatiḥ ।। 76

Upadraṣṭā Tathā Śreṣṭhaḥ Śucirbhūto Hyanāmayaḥ ।
Vedasiddhāntavedyaśca Mānasāhlādavardhanaḥ ।। 77

Dehadanyo Guṇādanyo Lokādanyo Vivekavit ।
Duṣṭasvapnaharaścaiva Gururguruvarottamaḥ ।। 78

Karmī Karmavinirmuktaḥ Saṃnyāsī Sādhakeśvaraḥ I
Sarvabhāvavihīnaśca Tṛṣṇāsaṅganivārakaḥ II 79

Tyāgī Tyāgavapustyāgastyāgadānavivarjitaḥ I
Tyāgakāraṇatyāgātmā Sadguruḥ Sukhadāyakaḥ II 80

Dakṣo Dakṣādivandyaśca Jñānavādapravartakaḥ I
Śabdabrahmamayātmā Ca Śabdabrahmaprakāśavān II 81

Grasiṣṇuḥ Prabhaviṣṇuśca Sahiṣṇurvigatāntaraḥ I
Vidvattamo Mahāvandyo Viśālottamavāṅmuniḥ II 82

Brahmavidbrahmabhāvaśca Brahmarṣirbāhmaṇapriyaḥ I
Brahma Brahmaprakāśātmā Brahmavidyāprakāśanaḥ II 83

Atrivaṃśaprabhūtātmā Tāpasottamavanditaḥ I
Ātmavāsī Vidheyātmā Hyatrivaṃśavivardhanaḥ II 84

Pravartano Nivṛttātmā Pralayodakasannibhaḥ I
Nārāyaṇo Mahāgarbho Bhārgavapriyakṛttamaḥ II 85

Saṅkalpaduḥkhadalanaḥ Saṃsāratamanāśanaḥ I
Trivikramastridhākārastrimūrtistriguṇātmakaḥ II 86

Bhedatrayaharaścaiva Tāpatrayanivārakaḥ I
Doṣatrayavibhedī Ca Saṃśayārṇavakhaṇḍanaḥ II 87

Asaṃśayastvasammūḍho Hyavādī Rājananditaḥ I
Rājayogī Mahāyogī Svabhāvagalitastathā II 88

Puṇyaślokaḥ Pavitrāṅghrirdhyānayogaparāyaṇaḥ I
Dhyānastho Dhyānagamyaśca Vidheyātmā Purātanaḥ II 89

Avijñeyo Hyantarātmā Mukhyabimbasanātanaḥ I
Jīvasañjīvano Jīvaścidvilāsaścidāśrayaḥ II 80

Mahendro'maramānyaśca Yogendro Yogavittamaḥ ।
Yogadharmastathā Yogastattvastattvaviniścayaḥ ।। 81

Naikabāhuranantātmā Naikanāmaparākramaḥ ।
Naikākṣī Naikapādaśca Nāthanāthottamottamaḥ ।। 82

Sahasraśīrṣā Puruṣaḥ Sahasrākṣaḥ Sahasrapāt ।
Sahasrarūpadṛkcaiva Sahasrāramayoddhavaḥ ।। 83

Tripādapuruṣaścaiva Tripādūrdhvastathaiva Ca ।
Tryambakaśca Mahāvīryo Yogavīryaviśāradaḥ ।। 84

Vijayī Vinayī Jetā Vītarāgī Virājitaḥ ।
Rudro Raudro Mahābhīmaḥ Prājñamukhyaḥ Sadāśuciḥ ।। 85

Antarjyotiranantātmā Pratyagātmā Nirantaraḥ ।
Arūpaścātmarūpaśca Sarvabhāvavinirvṛtaḥ ।। 86

Antaḥ Śūnyo Bahiḥ Śūnyaḥ Śūnyātmā Śūnyabhāvanaḥ ।
Antaḥpūrṇo Bahiḥpūrṇaḥ Pūrṇātmā Pūrṇabhāvanaḥ ।। 87

Antastyāgī Bahistyāgī Tyāgātmā Sarvayogavān ।
Antaryāgī Bahiryāgī Sarvayogaparāyaṇaḥ ।। 88

Antarbhogī Bahirbhogī Sarvabhogaviduttamaḥ ।
Antarniṣṭho Bahirniṣṭhaḥ Sarvaniṣṭhāmayastathā ।। 89

Bāhyāntaravimuktaśca Bāhyāntaravivarjitaḥ ।
Śāntaḥ Śuddho Viśuddhaśca Nirvāṇaḥ Prakṛteḥ Paraḥ ।। 100

Akālaḥ Kālanemī Ca Kālakālo Janeśvaraḥ ।
Kālātmā Kālakartā Ca Kālajñaḥ Kālanāśanaḥ ।। 101

Kaivalyapadadātā Ca Kaivalyasukhadāyakaḥ ।
Kaivalyakalanādhāro Nirbharo Harṣavardhanaḥ ।। 102

Hṛdayastho Hṛṣīkeśo Govindo Garbhavarjitaḥ |

Sakalāgamapūjyaśca Nigamo Nigamāśrayaḥ || 103

Parāśaktiḥ Parākīrtiḥ Parāvṛttirnidhismṛtiḥ |

Parāvidyā Parākṣāntirvibhaktiryuktasadgatiḥ || 104

Svaprakāśaḥ Prakāśātmā Parasaṃvedanātmakaḥ |

Svasevyaḥ Svavidāṃ Svātmā Svasaṃvedyo'naghaḥ Kṣamī || 105

Svānusandhānaśīlātmā Svānusandhānagocaraḥ |

Svānusandhānaśūnyātmā Svānusandhānāśrayastathā || 106

Svabodhadarpaṇo'bhaṅgaḥ Kandarpakulanāśanaḥ |

Brahmacārī Brahmavettā Brāhmaṇo Brahmavittamaḥ || 107

Tattvabodhaḥ Sudhāvarṣaḥ Pāvanaḥ Pāpapāvakaḥ |

Brahmasūtravidheyātmā Brahmasūtrārdhanirṇayaḥ || 108

Ātyantiko Mahākalpaḥ Saṅkalpāvartanāśanaḥ |

Ādhivyādhiharaścaiva Saṃśayārṇavaśoṣakaḥ || 109

Tattvātmajñānasandeśo Mahānubhavabhāvitaḥ |

Ātmānubhavasampannaḥ Svānubhāvasukhāśrayaḥ || 110

Acintyaśca Bṛhadbhānuḥ Pramadotkarṣanāśanaḥ |

Aniketapraśāntātmā Śūnyavāso Jagadvapuḥ || 111

Cidgatiścinmayaścakrī Māyācakrapravartakaḥ |

Sarvavarṇavidārambhī Sarvārambhaparāyaṇaḥ || 112

Purāṇaḥ Pravaro Dātā Sundaraḥ Kanakāṅgadī |

Anisūyātmajo Dattaḥ Sarvajñaḥ Sarvakāmadaḥ || 113

Kāmajitkāmapālaśca Kāmī Kāmapradāgamaḥ |

Kāmavānkāmapoṣaśca Sarvakāmanivartakaḥ || 114

Sarvakarmaphalotpattiḥ Sarvakāmaphalapradaḥ I
Sarvakarmaphalaiḥ Pūjyaḥ Sarvakarmaphalāśrayaḥ II 115

Viśvakarmā Kṛtātmā Ca Kṛtajñaḥ Sarvasākṣikaḥ I
Sarvārambhaparityāgī Jaḍonmattapiśācavān II 116

Bhikṣurbhikṣākaraścaiva Bhaikṣāhārī Nirāśramī I
Akūlaścānukūlaśca Vikalo Hyakalastathā II 117

Jaṭilo Vanacārī Ca Daṇḍī Muṇḍī Ca Gaṇḍavān I
Dehadharmavihīnātmā Hyekākī Saṅgavarjitaḥ II 118

Āśramyanāśramārambho'nācārī Karmavarjitaḥ I
Asandehī Ca Sandehī Na Kiñcinna Ca Kiñcanaḥ II 119

Nṛdehī Dehaśūnyaśca Nābhāvī Bhāvanirgataḥ I
Nābrahmaca Parabrahma Svayameva Nirākulaḥ II 120

Anaghaścāguruścaiva Nāthanāthottamo Guruḥ I
Dvibhujaḥ Prākṛtaścaiva Janakaśca Pitāmahaḥ II 121

Anātmā Na Ca Nānātmā Nītirnītimatāṃ Varaḥ I
Sahajaḥ Sadṛśaḥ Siddhaścaikaścinmātra Eva Ca II 122

Na Kartāpi Ca Kartā Ca Bhoktā Bhogavivarjitaḥ I
Turīyasturīyātītaḥ Svacchaḥ Sarvamayastathā II 123

Sarvādhiṣṭhānarūpaśca Sarvadhyeyavivarjitaḥ I
Sarvalokanivāsātmā Sakalottamavanditaḥ II 124

Dehabhṛddehakṛccaiva Dehātmā Dehabhāvanaḥ I
Dehī Dehavibhaktaśca Dehabhāvaprakāśanaḥ II 125

Layastho Layaviccaiva Layābhāvaśca Bodhavān I
Layātīto Layasyānto Layabhāvanivāraṇaḥ II 126

Vimukhaḥ Pramukhaścaiva Pratyaṅmukhavadācarī |
Viśvabhugviśvadhṛgviśvo Viśvakṣemakarastatjā || 127

Avikṣipto'pramādī Ca Pararddhiḥ Paramārthadṛk |
Svānubhāvavihīnaśca Svānubhāvaprakāśanaḥ || 128

Nirindriyaśca Nirbuddhirnirābhāso Nirākṛtaḥ |
Nirahaṅkāraścarūpātmā Nirvapuḥ Sakalāśrayaḥ || 129

Śokaduḥkhaharaścaiva Bhogamokṣaphalapradaḥ |
Suprasannastathā Sūkṣmaḥ Śabdabrahmārthasaṅgrahaḥ || 130

Āgamāpāyaśūnyaśca Sthānadaśca Satāṅgatiḥ |
Akṛtaḥ Sukṛtaścaiva Kṛtakarmā Vinirvṛtaḥ || 131

Bhedatrayavaraścaiva Dehatrayavinirgataḥ |
Sarvakāmamayaścaiva Sarvakāmanivartakaḥ || 132

Siddheśvaro'jaraḥ Pañcabāṇadarpahutāśanaḥ |
Caturakṣarabījātmā Svabhūścitkīrtibhūṣaṇaḥ || 133

Agādhabuddhirakṣubdhaścandrasūryāgnilocanaḥ |
Yamadaṃṣṭro'tisaṃhartā Paramānandasāgaraḥ || 134

Līlāviśvambharo Bhānurbhairavo Bhīmalocanaḥ |
Brahmacaryāmbaraḥ Kālastvacalaścalanāntakaḥ || 135

Ādidevo Jagadyonirvāsavārivimardanaḥ |
Vikarmakarmakarmajño'nanyagamako'gamaḥ || 136

Abaddhakarmaśūnyaśca Kāmarāgakulakṣayaḥ |
Yogāndhakāramathanaḥ Padmajanmādivanditaḥ || 137

Bhaktakāmo'grajaścakrī Bhāvanirbhāvabhāvakaḥ |
Bhedāntako Mahānagryo Nigūho Gocarāntakaḥ || 138

Kālāgniśamanaḥ Śaṅkhacakrapadmagadādharaḥ ।
Dīpto Dīnapatiḥ Śāstā Svacchando Muktidāyakaḥ ।। 139

Vyomadharmāmbaro Bhettā Bhasmadhārī Dharādharaḥ ।
Dharmagupto'nvayātmā Ca Vyatirekārthanirṇayaḥ ।। 140

Ekānekaguṇābhāsābhāsanirbhāsavarjitaḥ ।
Bhāvābhāvasvabhāvātmā Bhāvābhāvavibhāvavit ।। 141

Yogihṛdayaviśrāmo'nantavidyāvivardhanaḥ ।
Vighnāntakastrikālajñastattvātmā Jñānasāgaraḥ ।। 142

Phalaśrutiḥ ।

Nāmarūpātmakaṃ Caiva Avāṅmānasa Gocaraṃ ।
Sarvaṃ Dattātmakaṃ Viśvaṃ Bhāvābhāvodbhavātmakam ।। 143

Iti Śrī Paramaṃ Divyaṃ Pavitraṃ Pāpanāśanam ।
Dattātreyasahasrākhyaṃ Nāmastotraṃ Kṛtaṃ Mayā ।। 144

Atītānāgataṃ Caiva Vartamānaṃ Tadhaiva Ca ।
Tadvidurye Paṭhaṃ Tyetat Guhyādguhyataraṃ Param ।। 145

Śṛtvedaṃ Paramaṃ Puṇyaṃ Martyo Hyamṛtamaśnute ।
Sahasranāmakaṃ Stotraṃ Śraddhayā Parayā Bhuvi ।। 146

Idaṃ Stotramupāśritya Martyaścātmani Saṃsthitaḥ ।
Paraṃsthānamavāpnoti Śaṅkaraṃ Prakṛte Param ।। 147

Ekaikamakṣaraṃ Puṃsāṃ Maṇimādyaṣṭasiddhidam ।
Sarvapāpaharaṃ Caiva Brahmanirvāṇadāyakam ।। 148

Śivaṃ Pūrṇaṃ Paraṃ Caiva Nityaṃ Śuddhaṃ Nirañjanam ।
Nidhānaṃ Paramaṃ Divyaṃ Dattātreyaṃ Jagadgurum ।। 149

Nirīhaṃ Pratimāśūnyaṃ Satvagaṃ Gaganopamam I
Viśuddhamakṣaraṃ Pūrṇaṃ Dattātreyaṃ Jagadgurum I I 150

Avācyaṃ Praṇavātītaṃ Niṣprapañcaṃ Nirākalam I
Satyaṃ Siddhaṃ Mano'gamyaṃ Dattātreyaṃ Jagadgurum I I 151

Kāraṇaṃ Kāraṇānāṃ Ca Nāmarūpavivarjitam I
Paramaṃ Paramānandaṃ Dattātreyaṃ Jagadguram I I 152

Śāśvataṃ Sahajaṃ Śāntaṃ Pavitraṃ Ca Guṇātigam I
Satyaṃ Sanātanaṃ Sūkṣmaṃ Dattātreyaṃ Jagadguram I I 153

Nirākāraṃ Nirābhāsaṃ Niṣkalaṅkaṃ Nirāmayam I
Nirālambaṃ Nijānandaṃ Dattātreyaṃ Jagadguram I I 154

Deśakālārthanirmuktaṃ Deśakālasamāśrayam I
Parāparavinirmuktaṃ Dattātreyaṃ Jagadguram I I 155

Nigīśvaraṃ Nirvikāraṃ Nirmalajñānarūpiṇam I
Guṇādanyamahaṃ Vande Dattātreyaṃ Jagadguram I I 156

Ya Idaṃ Paṭhate Nityaṃ Pāṭhayedvāsamāhita I
Sarvānkāmānavāpnoti Dattātreyo Prasādataḥ I I 157

Itīdaṃ Dattasāhasraṃ Sāyaṃ Prātaḥ Paṭhettu Yaḥ I
Sa Ihāmutra Labhate Nirvāṇaṃ Paramaṃ Sukham I I 158

Guruvāre Dattabhakto Bhaktibhāvasamanvitaḥ I
Paṭhetsadaiva To Hyetatsa Labheccintitaṃ Dhruvam I I 159

Iti Śrī Brahmāṇḍa Purāṇe Anukūlāgame Sanatkumāra Brahmarṣi Saṃvāde Śrī Dattātreya Sahasranāma Stotraṃ Saṃpūrṇam II

श्री दत्तात्रेय सहस्रनाम स्तोत्रम् ॥

निखिलागमतत्त्वज्ञ ब्रह्मज्ञानपरायण । वदास्माकं मुक्त्युपायं सूत सर्वोपकारकम् ॥ १

सर्वदेवेषु को देवः सद्यो मोक्षप्रदो भवेत् ।
को मनुर्वा भवेत्तस्य सद्यः प्रीतिकरो ध्रुवम् ॥ २

सूत उवाच –

निगमागमतत्त्वज्ञो ह्यवधूतश्चिदम्बरः । भक्तवात्सल्यप्रवणो दत्त एव हि केवलः ॥ ३

सदा प्रसन्नवदनो भक्तचिन्तैकतत्परः ।
तस्य नामान्यनन्तानि वर्तन्तेऽथाप्यदः परम् ॥ ४

दत्तस्य नामसाहस्रं तस्य प्रीतिविवर्धनम् । यस्त्विदं पठते नित्यं दत्तात्रेयैकमानसः ॥ ५

मुच्यते सर्वपापेभ्यः स सस्द्यो नात्र संशयः ।
अन्ते तद्धाम संयाति पुनरावृत्तिदुर्लभम् ॥ ६

अस्य श्रीमद्दत्तात्रेयसहस्रनामस्तोत्रमन्त्रस्य अवधूत ऋषिः ।
अनुष्टुप्छन्दः । दिगम्बरो देवता । ॐ बीजम् । ह्रीं शक्तिः ।
क्रौं कीलकम् । श्रीदत्तात्रेयप्रीत्यर्थे जपे विनियोगः ॥

ध्यानम् ।

दिगम्बरं भस्मविलेपिताङ्गं बोधात्मकं मुक्तिकरं पर्सन्नम् ।
निर्मानसं श्यामतनुं भजेऽहं दत्तात्रेयं ब्रह्मसमाधियुक्तम् ॥

सहस्रनाम स्तोत्रम् ।

दत्तात्रेयो महोयोगी योगेशश्चामरप्रभुम् । मुनिर्दिगम्बरो बालो मायामुक्तो मदापहः ॥ १

अवधूतो महानाथः शङ्करोऽमरवल्लभः । महादेवश्चादिदेवः पुराणप्रभुरीश्वरः ॥ २

सत्त्वकृत्सत्त्वभृद्भावः सत्त्वात्मा सत्त्वसागरः ।
सत्त्ववित्सत्त्वसाक्षी च सत्त्वसाध्योऽमराधिपः ॥ ३

भूतकृद्भूतभृच्चैव भूतात्मा भूतसम्भवः ।भूतभावो भवो भूतवित्तथा भूतकारणः ॥ ४

भूतसाक्षी प्रभूतिश्च भूतानां परमा गतिः ।
भूतसङ्गविहीनात्मा भूतात्मा भूतशङ्करः ॥ ५

भूतनाथो महानाथश्चादिनाथो महेश्वरः । सर्वभूतनिवासात्मा भूतसन्तापनाशनः ॥ ६

सर्वात्मा सर्वभृत्सर्वः सर्वज्ञः सर्वनिर्णयः ।
सर्वसाक्षी बृहद्भानुः सर्ववित्सर्वमङ्गलः ॥ ७

शान्तः सत्यः समः पूर्णो ह्येकाकी कमलापतिः ।
रामो रामप्रियश्चैव विरामो रामकारणम् ॥ ८

शुद्धात्मा पावनोऽनन्तः प्रतीतः परमार्थभृत् ।
हंससाक्षी विभुश्चैव प्रभुः प्रलय इत्यपि ॥ ९

सिद्धात्मा परमात्मा च सिद्धानां परमा गतिः ।
सिद्धिसिद्धस्तथा साध्यः साधनो ह्युत्तमस्तथा ॥ १०

सुलक्षणः सुमेधावी विद्यावान्विगतान्तरः । विज्वरश्च महाबाहुर्बहुलानन्दवर्धनः ॥ ११

अव्यक्तपुरुषः प्राज्ञः परज्ञः परमार्थदृक् । परापरविनिर्मुक्तो युक्तस्तत्त्वप्रकाशवान् ॥ १२

दयावान्भगवान्भावी भावात्मा भावकारणः ।
भवसन्तापनाशश्च पुष्पवान्पण्डितो बुधः ॥ १३

प्रत्यक्षवस्तुर्विश्वात्मा प्रत्यग्ब्रह्म सनातनः । प्रमाणविगतश्चैव प्रत्याहारनियोजकः ॥ १४

प्रणवः प्रणवातीतः प्रमुखः प्रलयात्मकः ।
मृत्युञ्जयो विविक्तात्मा शङ्करात्मा परो वपुः ॥ १५

परमस्तनुविज्ञेयः परमात्मनि संस्थितः । प्रबोधकलनाधारः प्रभावप्रवरोत्तमः ॥ १६

चिदम्बरश्चिद्विलासश्चिदाकाशश्चिदुत्तमः ।
चित्तचैतन्यचित्तात्मा देवानां परमा गतिः ॥ १७

अचेत्यश्चेतनाधारश्चेतनाचित्तविक्रमः ।
चित्तात्मा चेतनारूपो लसत्पङ्कजलोचनः ॥ १८

परब्रह्म परं ज्योतिः परं धाम परन्तपः । परं सूत्रं परं तन्त्रं पवित्रं परमोहवान् ॥ १९

क्षेत्रज्ञः क्षेत्रगः क्षेत्रः क्षेत्राधारः पुरञ्जनः ।
क्षेत्रशून्यो लोकसाक्षी क्षेत्रवान्बहुनायकः ॥ २०

योगेन्दो योगपूज्यश्च योग आत्मविदां शुचिः ।
योगमायाधरः स्थाणुरचलः कमलापतिः ॥ २१

योगेशो योगनिर्माता योगज्ञानप्रकाशनः ।
योगपालो लोकपालः संसारतमनाशनः ॥ २२

गुह्यो गुह्यतमो गुप्तो मुक्तो युक्तः सनातनः ।
गहनो गगनाकारो गम्भीरो गणनायकः ॥ २३

गोविन्दो गोपतिर्गोप्ता गोभागो भावसंस्थितः ।
गोसाक्षी गोतमारिश्च गान्धारो गगनाकृतिः ॥ २४

योगयुक्तो भोगयुक्तः शङ्कामुक्तसमाधिमान् ।
सहजः सकलेशानः कार्तवीर्यवरप्रदः ॥ २५

सरजा विरजाः पुंसो पावनः पापनाशनः ।
पुमान् परावरविनिर्मुक्तः परञ्ज्योतिः पुरातनः ॥ २६

नानाज्योतिरनेकात्मा स्वयञ्ज्योतिः सदाशिवः ।
दिव्यज्योतिर्मयश्चैव सत्यविज्ञानभास्करः ॥ २७

नित्यशुद्धः परः पूर्णः प्रकाशः प्रकटोद्भवः ।प्रमादविगतश्चैव परेशः परविक्रमः ॥ २८

योगी योगो योगपश्च योगाभ्यासप्रकाशनः ।
योक्ता मोक्ता विधाता च त्राता पाता निरायुध्यः ॥ २९

नित्यमुक्तो नित्ययुक्तः सत्यः सत्यपराक्रमः ।
सत्त्वशुद्धिकरः सत्त्वस्तथा सत्त्वम्भृतां गतिः ॥ ३०

श्रीधरः श्रीवपुः श्रीमान् श्रीनिवासोऽमरार्चितः ।
श्रीनिधिः श्रीपतिः श्रेष्ठः श्रेयस्कश्चरमाश्रयः ॥ ३१

त्यागी त्यागार्थसम्पन्नस्त्यागात्मा त्यागविग्रहः ।
त्यागलक्षणसिद्धात्मा त्यागज्ञस्त्यागकारणः ॥ ३२

भोगो भोक्ता तथा भोग्यो भोगसाधनकारणः ।
भोगी भोगार्थसम्पन्नो भोगज्ञानप्रकाशनः ॥ ३३

केवलः केशवः कृष्णः कंवासाः कमलालयः ।
कमलासनपूज्यश्च हरिरज्ञानखण्डनः ॥ ३४

महात्मा महदादिश्च महेशोत्तमवन्दितः ।
मनोबुद्धिविहीनात्मा मानात्मा मानवाधिपः ॥ ३५

भुवनेशो विभूतिश्च धृतिर्मेधा स्मृतिर्दया । दुःखदावानलो बुद्धः प्रबुद्धः परमेश्वरः ॥ ३६

कामहा क्रोधहा चैव दम्भदर्पमदापहः । अज्ञानपतिमिरारिश्च भवारिर्भुवनेश्वरः ॥ ३७

रूपकृद्रूपभृद्रूपी रूपात्मा रूपकारणः ।
रूपज्ञो रूपसाक्षी च नामरूपो गुणान्तकः ॥ ३८

अप्रमेयः प्रमेयश्च प्रमाणं प्रणवाश्रयः ।
प्रमाणरहितोऽचिन्त्यश्चेतनाविगतोऽजरः ॥ ३९

अक्षरोऽक्षरमुक्तश्च विज्वरो ज्वरनाशनः ।
विशिष्टो वित्तशास्त्री च दृष्टो दृष्टान्तवर्जितः ॥ ४०

गुणेशो गुणकायश्च गुणात्मा गणभावनः ।
अनन्तगुणसम्पन्नो गुणगर्भो गुणाधिपः ॥ ४१

गणेशो गुणनाथश्च गुणात्मा गणभावनः ।
गणबन्धुर्विवेकात्मा गुणयुक्तः पराक्रमी ॥ ४२

अतर्क्यः क्रतुरग्निश्च कृतज्ञः सफलाश्रयः ।
यज्ञश्च यज्ञफल्दो यज्ञ इज्योऽमरोत्तमः ॥ ४३

हिरण्यगर्भः श्रीगर्भः खगर्भः कुणपेश्वरः ।
मायागर्भो लोकगर्भः स्वयम्भूर्भुवनान्तकः ॥ ४४

निष्पापो निबिडो नन्दी बोधी बोधसमाश्रयः ।
बोधात्मा बोधनात्मा च भेदवैतण्डखण्डनः ॥ ४५

स्वाभाव्यो भावनिर्मुक्तो व्यक्तोऽव्यक्तसमाश्रयः ।
नित्यतृप्तो निराभासो निर्वाणः शरणः सुहृत् ॥ ४६

गुह्येशो गुणगम्भीरो गुणदोषनिवारणः ।गुणसङ्गविहीनश्च योगारेर्दर्पनाशनः ॥ ४७

आनन्दः परमानन्दः स्वानन्दसुखवर्धनः ।
सत्यानन्दश्चिदानन्दः सर्वानन्दपरायणः ॥ ४८

सद्रूपः सहजः सत्यः स्वानन्दः सुमनोहरः ।
सर्वः सर्वान्तरश्चैव पूर्वात्पूर्वतरस्तथा ॥ ४९

खमयः खपरः खादिः खम्ब्रह्म खतनुः खगः ।
खवासाः खविहीनश्च खनिधिः खपराश्रयः ॥ ५०

अनन्तश्चादिरूपश्च सूर्यमण्डलमध्यगः ।
अमोघः परमामोघः परोक्षः वरदः कविः ॥ ५१

विश्वचक्षुर्विश्वसाक्षी विश्वबाहुर्धनेश्वरः ।
धनञ्जयो महातेजास्तेजिष्ठस्तैजसः सुखी ॥ ५२

ज्योतिर्ज्योतिर्मयो जेता ज्योतिषां ज्योतिरात्मकः ।
ज्योतिषामपि ज्योतिश्च जनको जनमोहनः ॥ ५३

जितेन्द्रियो जितक्रोधो जितात्मा जितमानसः ।
जितसङ्गो जितप्राणो जितसंसारवासनः ॥ ५४

निर्वासनो निरालम्बो निर्योगक्षेमवर्जितः ।
निरीहो निरहङ्कारो निराशीर्निरुपाधिकः ॥ ५५

नित्यबोधो विविक्तात्मा विशुद्धोत्तमगौरवः ।
विद्यार्थी परमार्थी च श्रद्धार्थी साधनात्मकः ॥ ५६

प्रत्याहारी निराहारी सर्वाहारपरायणः ।
नित्यशुद्धो निराकाङ्क्षी पारायणपरायणः ॥ ५७

अणोरणुतरः सूक्ष्मः स्थूलः स्थूलतरस्तथा ।
एकस्तथाऽनेकरूपो विश्वरूपः सनातनः ॥ ५८

नैकरूपो विरूपात्मा नैकबोधमयोऽपि च।
नैकनाममयश्चैव नैकविद्याविवर्धनः॥ ५९

एकश्चैकान्तिकश्चैव नानाभावविवर्जितः।
एकाक्षरस्तथा बीजः पूर्णबिम्बः सनातनः॥ ६०

मन्त्रवीर्यो मन्त्रबीजः शास्त्रवीर्यो जगत्पतिः।
नानावीर्यधरश्चैव शक्रेशः पृथिवीपतिः॥ ६१

प्राणेशः प्राणदः प्राणः प्राणायामपरायणः।
प्राणपञ्चकनिर्मुक्तः कोशपञ्चकवर्जितः॥ ६२

निश्चलो निष्कलोऽसङ्गो निष्प्रपञ्चो निरामयः।
निराधारो निराकारो निर्विकारो निरञ्जनः॥ ६३

निष्प्रतीतो निराभासो निरासक्तो निराकुलः।
निष्ठासर्वगतश्चैव निरारम्भो निराश्रयः॥ ६४

निरन्तरः सत्त्वगोप्ता शान्तो दान्तो महामुनिः।
निःशब्दः सुकृतः स्वस्थः सत्यवादी सुरेश्वरः॥ ६५

ज्ञानदो ज्ञानविज्ञानी ज्ञानात्माऽऽनन्दपूरितः।
ज्ञानयज्ञविदां दक्षो ज्ञानाग्निर्ज्वलनो बुधः॥ ६६

दयावान्भवरोगारिश्चिकित्साचरमागतिः।
चन्द्रमण्डलमध्यस्थश्चन्द्रकोटिसुशीतलः॥ ६७

यन्तकृत्परमो यन्त्री यन्त्रारूढपराजितः। यन्त्रविद्यन्त्रवासश्च यन्त्राधारो धराधरः॥ ६८

तत्त्वज्ञस्तत्त्वभूतात्मा महत्तत्त्वप्रकाशनः।
तत्त्वसङ्ख्यानयोगज्ञः साङ्ख्यशास्त्रप्रवर्तकः॥ ६९

अनन्तविक्रमो देवो माधवश्च धनेश्वरः।
साधुः साधुवरिष्ठात्मा सावधानोऽमरोत्तमः॥ ७०

निःसङ्कल्पो निराधारो दुर्धरो ह्यात्मवित्पतिः।
आरोग्यसुखदश्चैव प्रवरो वासवस्तथा॥ ७१

परेशः परमोदारः प्रत्यक्चैतन्यदुर्गमः । दुराधर्षो दुरावासो दूरत्वपरिनाशनः ॥ ७२

वेदविद्वेदकृद्वेदो वेदात्मा विमलाशयः । विविक्तसेवी च संसारश्रमनाशनस्तथा ॥ ७३

ब्रह्मयोनिर्बृहद्योनिर्विश्वयोनिर्विदेहवान् ।
विशालाक्षो विश्वनाथो हाटकाङ्गदभूषणः ॥ ७४

अबाध्यो जगदाराध्यो जगदार्जवपालनः ।
जनवान्धनवान्धर्मी धर्मगो धर्मवर्धनः ॥ ७५

अमृतः शाश्वतः साध्यः सिद्धिदः सुमनोहरः ।
खलुब्रह्मखलुस्थानो मुनीनां परमा गतिः ॥ ७६

उपद्रष्टा तथा श्रेष्ठः शुचिर्भूतो ह्यनामयः । वेदसिद्धान्तवेद्यश्च मानसाह्लादवर्धनः ॥ ७७

देहदन्यो गुणादन्यो लोकादन्यो विवेकवित् ।
दुष्टस्वप्नहरश्चैव गुरुर्गुरुवरोत्तमः ॥ ७८

कर्मी कर्मविनिर्मुक्तः संन्यासी साधकेश्वरः ।
सर्वभावविहीनश्च तृष्णासङ्गनिवारकः ॥ ७९

त्यागी त्यागवपुस्त्यागस्त्यागदानविवर्जितः ।
त्यागकारणत्यागात्मा सद्गुरुः सुखदायकः ॥ ८०

दक्षो दक्षादिवन्द्यश्च ज्ञानवादप्रवर्तकः ।
शब्दब्रह्ममयात्मा च शब्दब्रह्मप्रकाशवान् ॥ ८१

ग्रसिष्णुः प्रभविष्णुश्च सहिष्णुर्विगतान्तरः ।
विद्वत्तमो महावन्द्यो विशालोत्तमवाङ्मुनिः ॥ ८२

ब्रह्मविद्ब्रह्मभावश्च ब्रह्मर्षिर्ब्राह्मणप्रियः ।
ब्रह्म ब्रह्मप्रकाशात्मा ब्रह्मविद्याप्रकाशनः ॥ ८३

अत्रिवंशप्रभूतात्मा तापसोत्तमवन्दितः ।
आत्मवासी विधेयात्मा ह्यत्रिवंशविवर्धनः ॥ ८४

प्रवर्तनो निवृत्तात्मा प्रलयोदकसन्निभः ।
नारायणो महागर्भो भार्गवप्रियकृत्तमः ॥ ८५

सङ्कल्पदुःखदलनः संसारतमनाशनः ।
त्रिविक्रमस्त्रिधाकारस्त्रिमूर्तिस्त्रिगुणात्मकः ॥ ८६

भेदत्रयहरश्चैव तापत्रयनिवारकः । दोषत्रयविभेदी च संशयार्णवखण्डनः ॥ ८७

असंशयस्त्वसम्मूढो ह्यवादी राजनन्दितः ।
राजयोगी महायोगी स्वभावगलितस्तथा ॥ ८८

पुण्यश्लोकः पवित्राङ्घ्रिर्ध्यानयोगपरायणः ।
ध्यानस्थो ध्यानगम्यश्च विधेयात्मा पुरातनः ॥ ८९

अविज्ञेयो ह्यन्तरात्मा मुख्यबिम्बसनातनः ।
जीवसञ्जीवनो जीवश्चिद्विलासश्चिदाश्रयः ॥ ९०

महेन्द्रोऽमरमान्यश्च योगेन्द्रो योगवित्तमः ।
योगधर्मस्तथा योगस्तत्त्वस्तत्त्वविनिश्चयः ॥ ९१

नैकबाहुरनन्तात्मा नैकनामपराक्रमः । नैकाक्षी नैकपादश्च नाथनाथोत्तमोत्तमः ॥ ९२

सहस्रशीर्षा पुरुषः सहस्राक्षः सहस्रपात् ।सहस्ररूपदृक्चैव सहस्रारमयोद्भवः ॥ ९३

त्रिपादपुरुषश्चैव त्रिपादूर्ध्वस्तथैव च । त्र्यम्बकश्च महावीर्यो योगवीर्यविशारदः ॥ ९४

विजयी विनयी जेता वीतरागी विराजितः ।
रुद्रो रौद्रो महाभीमः प्राज्ञमुख्यः सदाशुचिः ॥ ९५

अन्तर्ज्योतिरनन्तात्मा प्रत्यगात्मा निरन्तरः ।
अरूपश्चात्मरूपश्च सर्वभावविनिर्वृतः ॥ ९६

अन्तः शून्यो बहिः शून्यः शून्यात्मा शून्यभावनः ।
अन्तःपूर्णो बहिःपूर्णः पूर्णात्मा पूर्णभावनः ॥ ९७

अन्तस्त्यागी बहिस्त्यागी त्यागात्मा सर्वयोगवान् ।
अन्तर्यागी बहिर्यागी सर्वयोगपरायणः ॥ ९८

अन्तर्भोगी बहिर्भोगी सर्वभोगविदुत्तमः ।
अन्तर्निष्ठो बहिर्निष्ठः सर्वनिष्ठामयस्तथा ॥ ९९

बाह्यान्तरविमुक्तश्च बाह्यान्तरविवर्जितः ।
शान्तः शुद्धो विशुद्धश्च निर्वाणः प्रकृतेः परः ॥ १००

अकालः कालनेमी च कालकालो जनेश्वरः ।
कालात्मा कालकर्ता च कालज्ञः कालनाशनः ॥ १०१

कैवल्यपददाता च कैवल्यसुखदायकः ।
कैवल्यकलनाधारो निर्भरो हर्षवर्धनः ॥ १०२

हृदयस्थो हृषीकेशो गोविन्दो गर्भवर्जितः ।
सकलागमपूज्यश्च निगमो निगमाश्रयः ॥ १०३

पराशक्तिः पराकीर्तिः परावृत्तिर्निधिस्मृतिः ।
पराविद्या पराक्षान्तिर्विभक्तिर्युक्तसद्गतिः ॥ १०४

स्वप्रकाशः प्रकाशात्मा परसंवेदनात्मकः ।
स्वसेव्यः स्वविदां स्वात्मा स्वसंवेद्योऽनघः क्षमी ॥ १०५

स्वानुसन्धानशीलात्मा स्वानुसन्धानगोचरः ।
स्वानुसन्धानशून्यात्मा स्वानुसन्धानाश्रयस्तथा ॥ १०६

स्वबोधदर्पणोऽभङ्गः कन्दर्पकुलनाशनः ।
ब्रह्मचारी ब्रह्मवेत्ता ब्राह्मणो ब्रह्मवित्तमः ॥ १०७

तत्त्वबोधः सुधावर्षः पावनः पापपावकः ।
ब्रह्मसूत्रविधेयात्मा ब्रह्मसूत्रार्धनिर्णयः ॥ १०८

आत्यन्तिको महाकल्पः सङ्कल्पावर्तनाशनः ।
आधिव्याधिहरश्चैव संशयार्णवशोषकः ॥ १०९

तत्त्वात्मज्ञानसन्देशो महानुभवभावितः ।
आत्मानुभवसम्पन्नः स्वानुभावसुखाश्रयः ॥ ११०

अचिन्त्यश्च बृहद्भानुः प्रमदोत्कर्षनाशनः ।
अनिकेतप्रशान्तात्मा शून्यवासो जगद्वपुः ॥ १११

चिद्गतिश्चिन्मयश्चक्री मायाचक्रप्रवर्तकः ।
सर्ववर्णविदारम्भी सर्वारम्भपरायणः ॥ ११२

पुराणः प्रवरो दाता सुन्दरः कनकाङ्गदी ।
अनिसूयात्मजो दत्तः सर्वज्ञः सर्वकामदः ॥ ११३

कामजित्कामपालश्च कामी कामप्रदागमः ।
कामवान्कामपोषश्च सर्वकामनिवर्तकः ॥ ११४

सर्वकर्मफलोत्पत्तिः सर्वकामफलप्रदः ।
सर्वकर्मफलैः पूज्यः सर्वकर्मफलाश्रयः ॥ ११५

विश्वकर्मा कृतात्मा च कृतज्ञः सर्वसाक्षिकः ।
सर्वारम्भपरित्यागी जडोन्मत्तपिशाचवान् ॥ ११६

भिक्षुर्भिक्षाकरश्चैव भैक्षाहारी निराश्रमी ।
अकूलश्चानुकूलश्च विकलो ह्यकलस्तथा ॥ ११७

जटिलो वनचारी च दण्डी मुण्डी च गण्डवान् ।
देहधर्मविहीनात्मा ह्येकाकी सङ्गवर्जितः ॥ ११८

आश्रम्यनाश्रमारम्भोऽनाचारी कर्मवर्जितः ।
असन्देही च सन्देही न किञ्चिन्न च किञ्चनः ॥ ११९

नृदेही देहशून्यश्च नाभावी भावनिर्गतः ।नाब्रह्मच परब्रह्म स्वयमेव निराकुलः ॥ १२०

अनघश्चागुरुश्चैव नाथनाथोत्तमो गुरुः । द्विभुजः प्राकृतश्चैव जनकश्च पितामहः ॥ १२१

अनात्मा न च नानात्मा नीतिर्नीतिमतां वरः ।
सहजः सदृशः सिद्धश्चैकश्चिन्मात्र एव च ॥ १२२

न कर्तापि च कर्ता च भोक्ता भोगविवर्जितः ।
तुरीयस्तुरीयातीतः स्वच्छः सर्वमयस्तथा ॥ १२३

सर्वाधिष्ठानरूपश्च सर्वध्येयविवर्जितः ।
सर्वलोकनिवासात्मा सकलोत्तमवन्दितः ॥ १२४

देहभृद्देहकृच्चैव देहात्मा देहभावनः । देही देहविभक्तश्च देहभावप्रकाशनः ॥ १२५

लयस्थो लयविच्चैव लयाभावश्च बोधवान् ।
लयातीतो लयस्यान्तो लयभावनिवारणः ॥ १२६

विमुखः प्रमुखश्चैव प्रत्यङ्मुखवदाचरी ।
विश्वभुग्विश्वधृग्विश्वो विश्वक्षेमकरस्तत्जा ॥ १२७

अविक्षिप्तोऽप्रमादी च परर्द्धिः परमार्थदृक् ।
स्वानुभावविहीनश्च स्वानुभावप्रकाशनः ॥ १२८

निरिन्द्रियश्च निर्बुद्धिर्निराभासो निराकृतः ।
निरहङ्कारश्चरूपात्मा निर्वपुः सकलाश्रयः ॥ १२९

शोकदुःखहरश्चैव भोगमोक्षफलप्रदः ।
सुप्रसन्नस्तथा सूक्ष्मः शब्दब्रह्मार्थसङ्ग्रहः ॥ १३०

आगमापायशून्यश्च स्थानदश्च सताङ्गतिः ।
अकृतः सुकृतश्चैव कृतकर्मा विनिर्वृतः ॥ १३१

भेदत्रयवरश्चैव देहत्रयविनिर्गतः । सर्वकाममयश्चैव सर्वकामनिवर्तकः ॥ १३२

सिद्धेश्वरोऽजरः पञ्चबाणदर्पहुताशनः ।
चतुरक्षरबीजात्मा स्वभूश्चित्कीर्तिभूषणः ॥ १३३

अगाधबुद्धिरक्षुब्धश्चन्द्रसूर्याग्निलोचनः ।यमदंष्ट्रोऽतिसंहर्ता परमानन्दसागरः ॥ १३४

लीलाविश्वम्भरो भानुर्भैरवो भीमलोचनः ।
ब्रह्मचर्याम्बरः कालस्त्वचलश्चलनान्तकः ॥ १३५

आदिदेवो जगद्योनिर्वासवारिविमर्दनः । विकर्मकर्मकर्मज्ञोऽनन्यगमकोऽगमः ॥ १३६

अबद्धकर्मशून्यश्च कामरागकुलक्षयः ।
योगान्धकारमथनः पद्मजन्मादिवन्दितः ॥ १३७

भक्तकामोऽग्रजश्चक्री भावनिर्भावभावकः ।
भेदान्तको महानग्र्यो निगूहो गोचरान्तकः ॥ १३८

कालाग्निशमनः शङ्खचक्रपद्मगदाधरः ।
दीप्तो दीनपतिः शास्ता स्वच्छन्दो मुक्तिदायकः ॥ १३९

व्योमधर्माम्बरो भेत्ता भस्मधारी धराधरः ।
धर्मगुप्तोऽन्वयात्मा च व्यतिरेकार्थनिर्णयः ॥ १४०

एकानेकगुणाभासाभासनिर्भासवर्जितः ।
भावाभावस्वभावात्मा भावाभावविभाववित् ॥ १४१

योगिहृदयविश्रामोऽनन्तविद्याविवर्धनः ।
विघ्नान्तकस्त्रिकालज्ञस्तत्त्वात्मा ज्ञानसागरः ॥ १४२

फलश्रुतिः ।

नामरूपात्मकं चैव अवाङ्मनस गोचरं ।
सर्वं दत्तात्मकं विश्वं भावाभावोद्भवात्मकम् ॥ १४३

इति श्री परमं दिव्यं पवित्रं पापनाशनम् ।
दत्तात्रेयसहस्राख्यं नामस्तोत्रं कृतं मया ॥ १४४

अतीतानागतं चैव वर्तमानं तथैव च ।
तद्विदुर्ये पठं त्येतत् गुह्याद्गु ह्यतरं परम् ॥ १४५

शृत्वेदं परमं पुण्यं मर्त्यो ह्यमृतमश्नुते ।
सहस्रनामकं स्तोत्रं श्रद्धया परया भुवि ॥ १४६

इदं स्तोत्रमुपाश्रित्य मर्त्यश्चात्मनि संस्थितः ।
परंस्थानमवाप्नोति शङ्करं प्रकृते परम् ॥ १४७

एकैकमक्षरं पुंसां मणिमाद्यष्टसिद्धिदम् ।
सर्वपापहरं चैव ब्रह्मनिर्वाणदायकम् ॥ १४८

शिवं पूर्णं परं चैव नित्यं शुद्धं निरञ्जनम् ।
निधानं परमं दिव्यं दत्तात्रेयं जगद्गु रुम् ॥ १४९

निरीहं प्रतिमाशून्यं सत्वगं गगनोपमम् ।विशुद्धमक्षरं पूर्णं दत्तात्रेयं जगद्गु रुम् ॥ १५०

अवाच्यं प्रणवातीतं निष्प्रपञ्चं निराकलम् ।
सत्यं सिद्धं मनोऽगम्यं दत्तात्रेयं जगद्गु रुम् ॥ १५१

कारणं कारणानां च नामरूपविवर्जितम् ।परमं परमानन्दं दत्तात्रेयं जगद्गु रम् ॥ १५२

शाश्वतं सहजं शान्तं पवित्रं च गुणातिगम् ।
सत्यं सनातनं सूक्ष्मं दत्तात्रेयं जगद्गु रम् ॥ १५३

निराकारं निराभासं निष्कलङ्कं निरामयम् ।
निरालम्बं निजानन्दं दत्तात्रेयं जगद्गुरुम् ॥ १५४

देशकालार्थनिर्मुक्तं देशकालसमाश्रयम् ।
परापरविनिर्मुक्तं दत्तात्रेयं जगद्गुरुम् ॥ १५५

निगीश्वरं निर्विकारं निर्मलज्ञानरूपिणम् ।गुणादन्यमहं वन्दे दत्तात्रेयं जगद्गुरुम् ॥ १५६

य इदं पठते नित्यं पाठयेद्वासमाहित ।
सर्वान्कामानवाप्नोति दत्तात्रेयो प्रसादतः ॥ १५७

इतीदं दत्तसाहस्रं सायं प्रातः पठेत्तु यः ।
स इहामुत्र लभते निर्वाणं परमं सुखम् ॥ १५८

गुरुवारे दत्तभक्तो भक्तिभावसमन्वितः ।
पठेत्सदैव तो ह्येतत्स लभेच्चिन्तितं ध्रुवम् ॥ १५९

इति श्री ब्रह्माण्डपुराणे अनुकूलागमे सनत्कुमारब्रह्मऋषि संवादे श्री दत्तात्रेय सहस्रनाम स्तोत्रं संपूर्णम् ॥

*****

Śrīmad Dattātreya Sahasra Nāmāvalī
श्रीमद् दत्तात्रेयसहस्रनामावली

1,000 divine names on *Dattatreya Deva* culminated from 142 shlokas of the the previous chapter *Śrī Dattātreya Sahasranāma Stotraṃ*;

1.	*Oṃ Śrī Dattātreyāya Namaḥ* I	ॐ श्री दत्तात्रेयाय नमः ।
2.	*Oṃ Mahāyogine Namaḥ* I	ॐ महायोगिने नमः ।
3.	*Oṃ Yogeśāya Namaḥ* I	ॐ योगेशाय नमः ।
4.	*Oṃ Amaraprabhave Namaḥ* I	ॐ अमरप्रभवे नमः ।
5.	*Oṃ Munaye Namaḥ* I	ॐ मुनये नमः ।
6.	*Oṃ Digambarāya Namaḥ* I	ॐ दिगम्बराय नमः ।
7.	*Oṃ Bālāya Namaḥ* I	ॐ बालाय नमः ।
8.	*Oṃ Māyāmuktāya Namaḥ* I	ॐ मायामुक्ताय नमः ।
9.	*Oṃ Madāpahāya Namaḥ* I	ॐ मदापहाय नमः ।
10.	*Oṃ Avadhūtāya Namaḥ* I	ॐ अवधूताय नमः ।
11.	*Oṃ Mahānāthāya Namaḥ* I	ॐ महानाथाय नमः ।
12.	*Oṃ Śaṅkarāya Namaḥ* I	ॐ शङ्कराय नमः ।
13.	*Oṃ Amaravallabhāya Namaḥ* I	ॐ अमरवल्लभाय नमः ।
14.	*Oṃ Mahādevāya Namaḥ* I	ॐ महादेवाय नमः ।
15.	*Oṃ Ādidevāya Namaḥ* I	ॐ आदिदेवाय नमः ।
16.	*Oṃ Purāṇaprabhave Namaḥ* I	ॐ पुराणप्रभवे नमः ।
17.	*Oṃ Īśvarāya Namaḥ* I	ॐ ईश्वराय नमः ।
18.	*Oṃ Sattvakṛte Namaḥ* I	ॐ सत्त्वकृते नमः ।
19.	*Oṃ Sattvabhṛte Namaḥ* I	ॐ सत्त्वभृते नमः ।
20.	*Oṃ Bhāvāya Namaḥ* I	ॐ भावाय नमः ।
21.	*Oṃ Sattvātmane Namaḥ* I	ॐ सत्त्वात्मने नमः ।
22.	*Oṃ Sattvasāgarāya Namaḥ* I	ॐ सत्त्वसागराय नमः ।
23.	*Oṃ Sattvavide Namaḥ* I	ॐ सत्त्वविदे नमः ।
24.	*Oṃ Sattvasākṣiṇe Namaḥ* I	ॐ सत्त्वसाक्षिणे नमः ।

25.	*Oṃ Sattvasādhyāya Namaḥ* I	ॐ सत्त्वसाध्याय नमः।
26.	*Oṃ Amarādhipāya Namaḥ* I	ॐ अमराधिपाय नमः।
27.	*Oṃ Bhūtakṛte Namaḥ* I	ॐ भूतकृते नमः।
28.	*Oṃ Bhūtabhṛte Namaḥ* I	ॐ भूतभृते नमः।
29.	*Oṃ Bhūtātmane Namaḥ* I	ॐ भूतात्मने नमः।
30.	*Oṃ Bhūtasambhavāya Namaḥ* I	ॐ भूतसम्भवाय नमः।
31.	*Oṃ Bhūtabhavāya Namaḥ* I	ॐ भूतभवाय नमः।
32.	*Oṃ Bhāvāya Namaḥ* I	ॐ भावाय नमः।
33.	*Oṃ Bhūtavide Namaḥ* I	ॐ भूतविदे नमः।
34.	*Oṃ Bhūtakāraṇāya Namaḥ* I	ॐ भूतकारणाय नमः।
35.	*Oṃ Bhūtasākṣiṇe Namaḥ* I	ॐ भूतसाक्षिणे नमः।
36.	*Oṃ Prabhūtaye Namaḥ* I	ॐ प्रभूतये नमः।
37.	*Oṃ Bhūtānāṃ Paramaṃ Gataye Namaḥ* I	ॐ भूतानां परमं गतये नमः।
38.	*Oṃ Bhūtasaṅgavihīnātmane Namaḥ* I	ॐ भूतसङ्गविहीनात्मने नमः।
39.	*Oṃ Bhūtātmane Namaḥ* I	ॐ भूतात्मने नमः।
40.	*Oṃ Bhūtaśaṅkarāya Namaḥ* I	ॐ भूतशङ्कराय नमः।
41.	*Oṃ Bhūtanāthāya Namaḥ* I	ॐ भूतनाथाय नमः।
42.	*Oṃ Bhūtamahānāthāya Namaḥ* I	ॐ भूतमहानाथाय नमः।
43.	*Oṃ Bhūtādināthāya Namaḥ* I	ॐ भूतादिनाथाय नमः।
44.	*Oṃ Maheśvarāya Namaḥ* I	ॐ महेश्वराय नमः।
45.	*Oṃ Sarvabhūtanivāsātmane Namaḥ* I	ॐ सर्वभूतनिवासात्मने नमः।
46.	*Oṃ Bhūtasantāpanāśanāya Namaḥ* I	ॐ भूतसन्तापनाशनाय नमः।
47.	*Oṃ Sarvātmane Namaḥ* I	ॐ सर्वात्मने नमः।
48.	*Oṃ Sarvabhṛte Namaḥ* I	ॐ सर्वभृते नमः।

49.	*Oṃ Sarvāya Namaḥ* |	ॐ सर्वाय नमः ।
50.	*Oṃ Sarvajñāya Namaḥ* |	ॐ सर्वज्ञाय नमः ।
51.	*Oṃ Sarvanirṇayāya Namaḥ* |	ॐ सर्वनिर्णयाय नमः ।
52.	*Oṃ Sarvasākṣiṇe Namaḥ* |	ॐ सर्वसाक्षिणे नमः ।
53.	*Oṃ Bṛhadbhānave Namaḥ* |	ॐ बृहद्भानवे नमः ।
54.	*Oṃ Sarvavide Namaḥ* |	ॐ सर्वविदे नमः ।
55.	*Oṃ Sarvamaṅgalāya Namaḥ* |	ॐ सर्वमङ्गलाय नमः ।
56.	*Oṃ Śāntāya Namaḥ* |	ॐ शान्ताय नमः ।
57.	*Oṃ Satyāya Namaḥ* |	ॐ सत्याय नमः ।
58.	*Oṃ Śamāya Namaḥ* |	ॐ शमाय नमः ।
59.	*Oṃ Samāya Namaḥ* |	ॐ समाय नमः ।
60.	*Oṃ Ekākine Namaḥ* |	ॐ एकाकिने नमः ।
61.	*Oṃ Kamalāpataye Namaḥ* |	ॐ कमलापतये नमः ।
62.	*Oṃ Rāmāya Namaḥ* |	ॐ रामाय नमः ।
63.	*Oṃ Rāmapriyāya Namaḥ* |	ॐ रामप्रियाय नमः ।
64.	*Oṃ Virāmāya Namaḥ* |	ॐ विरामाय नमः ।
65.	*Oṃ Rāmakāraṇāya Namaḥ* |	ॐ रामकारणाय नमः ।
66.	*Oṃ Śuddhātmane Namaḥ* |	ॐ शुद्धात्मने नमः ।
67.	*Oṃ Pavanāya Namaḥ* |	ॐ पवनाय नमः ।
68.	*Oṃ Anantāya Namaḥ* |	ॐ अनन्ताय नमः ।
69.	*Oṃ Pratītāya Namaḥ* |	ॐ प्रतीताय नमः ।
70.	*Oṃ Paramārthabhṛte Namaḥ* |	ॐ परमार्थभृते नमः ।
71.	*Oṃ Haṃsasākṣiṇe Namaḥ* |	ॐ हंससाक्षिणे नमः ।
72.	*Oṃ Vibhave Namaḥ* |	ॐ विभवे नमः ।
73.	*Oṃ Prabhave Namaḥ* |	ॐ प्रभवे नमः ।
74.	*Oṃ Pralayāya Namaḥ* |	ॐ प्रलयाय नमः ।
75.	*Oṃ Siddhātmane Namaḥ* |	ॐ सिद्धात्मने नमः ।
76.	*Oṃ Paramātmane Namaḥ* |	ॐ परमात्मने नमः ।

77.	*Oṃ Siddhānāṃ Paramagataye Namaḥ* |	ॐ सिद्धानां परमगतये नमः ।
78.	*Oṃ Siddhisiddhaye Namaḥ* |	ॐ सिद्धिसिद्धये नमः ।
79.	*Oṃ Sādhyāya Namaḥ* |	ॐ साध्याय नमः ।
80.	*Oṃ Sādhanāya Namaḥ* |	ॐ साधनाय नमः ।
81.	*Oṃ Uttamāya Namaḥ* |	ॐ उत्तमाय नमः ।
82.	*Oṃ Sulakṣaṇāya Namaḥ* |	ॐ सुलक्षणाय नमः ।
83.	*Oṃ Sumedhāvine Namaḥ* |	ॐ सुमेधाविने नमः ।
84.	*Oṃ Vidyavate Namaḥ* |	ॐ विद्यवते नमः ।
85.	*Oṃ Vigatāntarāya Namaḥ* |	ॐ विगतान्तराय नमः ।
86.	*Oṃ Vijvarāya Namaḥ* |	ॐ विज्वराय नमः ।
87.	*Oṃ Mahābāhave Namaḥ* |	ॐ महाबाहवे नमः ।
88.	*Oṃ Bahulānandavardhanāya Namaḥ* |	ॐ बहुलानन्दवर्धनाय नमः ।
89.	*Oṃ Avyaktapuruṣāya Namaḥ* |	ॐ अव्यक्तपुरुषाय नमः ।
90.	*Oṃ Prajñāya Namaḥ* |	ॐ प्रज्ञाय नमः ।
91.	*Oṃ Parajñāya Namaḥ* |	ॐ परज्ञाय नमः ।
92.	*Oṃ Paramārthadṛśe Namaḥ* |	ॐ परमार्थदृशे नमः ।
93.	*Oṃ Parāparavinirmuktāya Namaḥ* |	ॐ परापरविनिर्मुक्ताय नमः ।
94.	*Oṃ Yuktāya Namaḥ* |	ॐ युक्ताय नमः ।
95.	*Oṃ Tattvaprakāśavate Namaḥ* |	ॐ तत्त्वप्रकाशवते नमः ।
96.	*Oṃ Dayāvate Namaḥ* |	ॐ दयावते नमः ।
97.	*Oṃ Bhagavate Namaḥ* |	ॐ भगवते नमः ।
98.	*Oṃ Bhāvine Namaḥ* |	ॐ भाविने नमः ।
99.	*Oṃ Bhāvātmane Namaḥ* |	ॐ भावात्मने नमः ।
100.	*Oṃ Bhāvakāraṇāya Namaḥ* |	ॐ भावकारणाय नमः ।
101.	*Oṃ Bhavasantāpanāśanāya* ||	ॐ भवसन्तापनाशनाय ॥

102.	*Oṃ Puṣpavate Namaḥ* |	ॐ पुष्पवते नमः ।
103.	*Oṃ Paṇḍitāya Namaḥ* |	ॐ पण्डिताय नमः ।
104.	*Oṃ Buddhāya Namaḥ* |	ॐ बुद्धाय नमः ।
105.	*Oṃ Pratyakṣavastave Namaḥ* |	ॐ प्रत्यक्षवस्तवे नमः ।
106.	*Oṃ Viśvātmane Namaḥ* |	ॐ विश्वात्मने नमः ।
107.	*Oṃ Pratyagbrahmasanātanāya Namaḥ* |	ॐ प्रत्यग्ब्रह्मसनातनाय नमः ।
108.	*Oṃ Pramāṇavigatāya Namaḥ* |	ॐ प्रमाणविगताय नमः ।
109.	*Oṃ Pratyāhāraṇī Yojakāya Namaḥ* |	ॐ प्रत्याहारणी योजकाय नमः ।
110.	*Oṃ Praṇavāya Namaḥ* |	ॐ प्रणवाय नमः ।
111.	*Oṃ Praṇavātītāya Namaḥ* |	ॐ प्रणवातीताय नमः ।
112.	*Oṃ Pramukhāya Namaḥ* |	ॐ प्रमुखाय नमः ।
113.	*Oṃ Pralayātmakāya Namaḥ* |	ॐ प्रलयात्मकाय नमः ।
114.	*Oṃ Mṛtyuñjayāya Namaḥ* |	ॐ मृत्युञ्जयाय नमः ।
115.	*Oṃ Viviktātmane Namaḥ* |	ॐ विविक्तात्मने नमः ।
116.	*Oṃ Śaṅkarātmane Namaḥ* |	ॐ शङ्करात्मने नमः ।
117.	*Oṃ Parasmaivapuṣe Namaḥ* |	ॐ परस्मैवपुषे नमः ।
118.	*Oṃ Paramāya Namaḥ* |	ॐ परमाय नमः ।
119.	*Oṃ Tanuvijñeyāya Namaḥ* |	ॐ तनुविज्ञेयाय नमः ।
120.	*Oṃ Paramātmanisaṃsthitāya Namaḥ* |	ॐ परमात्मनिसंस्थिताय नमः ।
121.	*Oṃ Prabodhakalanādhārāya Namaḥ* |	ॐ प्रबोधकलनाधाराय नमः ।
122.	*Oṃ Prabhāva Pravarottamāya Namaḥ* |	ॐ प्रभाव प्रवरोत्तमाय नमः ।
123.	*Oṃ Cidambarāya Namaḥ* |	ॐ चिदम्बराय नमः ।
124.	*Oṃ Cidvilāsāya Namaḥ* |	ॐ चिद्विलासाय नमः ।
125.	*Oṃ Cidākāśāya Namaḥ* |	ॐ चिदाकाशाय नमः ।

126.	*Oṃ Ciduttamāya Namaḥ* |	ॐ चिदुत्तमाय नमः ।
127.	*Oṃ Citta Caitanya Cittātmane Namaḥ* |	ॐ चित्त चैतन्य चित्तात्मने नमः ।
128.	*Oṃ Devānāṃ Paramāgataye Namaḥ* |	ॐ देवानां परमागतये नमः ।
129.	*Oṃ Acetyāya Namaḥ* |	ॐ अचेत्याय नमः ।
130.	*Oṃ Cetanādhārāya Namaḥ* |	ॐ चेतनाधाराय नमः ।
131.	*Oṃ Cetanācittavikramāya Namaḥ* |	ॐ चेतनाचित्तविक्रमाय नमः ।
132.	*Oṃ Cittātmane Namaḥ* |	ॐ चित्तात्मने नमः ।
133.	*Oṃ Cetanārūpāya Namaḥ* |	ॐ चेतनारूपाय नमः ।
134.	*Oṃ Lasatpaṅkajalocanāya Namaḥ* |	ॐ लसत्पङ्कजलोचनाय नमः ।
135.	*Oṃ Parabrahmaṇe Namaḥ* |	ॐ परब्रह्मणे नमः ।
136.	*Oṃ Parañjyotiye Namaḥ* |	ॐ परञ्ज्योतिये नमः ।
137.	*Oṃ Parandhāmne Namaḥ* |	ॐ परन्धाम्ने नमः ।
138.	*Oṃ Parantapase Namaḥ* |	ॐ परन्तपसे नमः ।
139.	*Oṃ Paraṃsūtrāya Namaḥ* |	ॐ परंसूत्राय नमः ।
140.	*Oṃ Paratantrāya Namaḥ* |	ॐ परतन्त्राय नमः ।
141.	*Oṃ Pavitrāya Namaḥ* |	ॐ पवित्राय नमः ।
142.	*Oṃ Paramohavate Namaḥ* |	ॐ परमोहवते नमः ।
143.	*Oṃ Kṣetrajñāya Namaḥ* |	ॐ क्षेत्रज्ञाय नमः ।
144.	*Oṃ Kṣetragāya Namaḥ* |	ॐ क्षेत्रगाय नमः ।
145.	*Oṃ Kṣetrāya Namaḥ* |	ॐ क्षेत्राय नमः ।
146.	*Oṃ Kṣetrādhārāya Namaḥ* |	ॐ क्षेत्राधाराय नमः ।
147.	*Oṃ Purāñjyanāya Namaḥ* |	ॐ पुराञ्ज्यनाय नमः ।
148.	*Oṃ Kṣetraśūnyāya Namaḥ* |	ॐ क्षेत्रशून्याय नमः ।
149.	*Oṃ Lokasākṣiṇe Namaḥ* |	ॐ लोकसाक्षिणे नमः ।

150.	*Oṃ Kṣetravate Namaḥ* |	ॐ क्षेत्रवते नमः ।
151.	*Oṃ Bahunāyakāya Namaḥ* |	ॐ बहुनायकाय नमः ।
152.	*Oṃ Yogīndrāya Namaḥ* |	ॐ योगीन्द्राय नमः ।
153.	*Oṃ Yogapūjyāya Namaḥ* |	ॐ योगपूज्याय नमः ।
154.	*Oṃ Yogyāya Namaḥ* |	ॐ योग्याय नमः ।
155.	*Oṃ Ātmavidaṃśucaye Namaḥ* |	ॐ आत्मविदंशुचये नमः।
156.	*Oṃ Yogamāyādharāya Namaḥ* |	ॐ योगमायाधराय नमः ।
157.	*Oṃ Sthānave Namaḥ* |	ॐ स्थानवे नमः ।
158.	*Oṃ Acalāya Namaḥ* |	ॐ अचलाय नमः ।
159.	*Oṃ Kamalāpataye Namaḥ* |	ॐ कमलापतये नमः ।
160.	*Oṃ Yogeśāya Namaḥ* |	ॐ योगेशाय नमः ।
161.	*Oṃ Yoganimantre Namaḥ* |	ॐ योगनिमन्त्रे नमः ।
162.	*Oṃ Yogajñānaprakāśakāya Namaḥ* |	ॐ योगज्ञानप्रकाशकाय नमः ।
163.	*Oṃ Yogapālāya Namaḥ* |	ॐ योगपालाय नमः ।
164.	*Oṃ Lokapālāya Namaḥ* |	ॐ लोकपालाय नमः ।
165.	*Oṃ Saṃsāratamonāśanāya Namaḥ* |	ॐ संसारतमोनाशनाय नमः ।
166.	*Oṃ Guhyāya Namaḥ* |	ॐ गुह्याय नमः ।
167.	*Oṃ Guhyatamāya Namaḥ* |	ॐ गुह्यतमाय नमः ।
168.	*Oṃ Guptaye Namaḥ* |	ॐ गुप्तये नमः ।
169.	*Oṃ Muktāya Namaḥ* |	ॐ मुक्ताय नमः ।
170.	*Oṃ Yuktāya Namaḥ* |	ॐ युक्ताय नमः ।
171.	*Oṃ Sanātanāya Namaḥ* |	ॐ सनातनाय नमः ।
172.	*Oṃ Gahanāya Namaḥ* |	ॐ गहनाय नमः ।
173.	*Oṃ Gaganākārāya Namaḥ* |	ॐ गगनाकाराय नमः ।
174.	*Oṃ Gambhīrāya Namaḥ* |	ॐ गम्भीराय नमः ।
175.	*Oṃ Gaṇanāyakāya Namaḥ* |	ॐ गणनायकाय नमः ।

176.	*Oṃ Govindāya Namaḥ* ।	ॐ गोविन्दाय नमः ।
177.	*Oṃ Gopataye Namaḥ* ।	ॐ गोपतये नमः ।
178.	*Oṃ Goptre Namaḥ* ।	ॐ गोप्त्रे नमः ।
179.	*Oṃ Gobhāgāya Namaḥ* ।	ॐ गोभागाय नमः ।
180.	*Oṃ Bhāvasaṃsthitāya Namaḥ* ।	ॐ भावसंस्थिताय नमः ।
181.	*Oṃ Gosākṣiṇe Namaḥ* ।	ॐ गोसाक्षिणे नमः ।
182.	*Oṃ Gotamāraye Namaḥ* ।	ॐ गोतमारये नमः ।
183.	*Oṃ Gāndhārāya Namaḥ* ।	ॐ गान्धाराय नमः ।
184.	*Oṃ Gaganākṛtaye Namaḥ* ।	ॐ गगनाकृतये नमः ।
185.	*Oṃ Yogayuktāya Namaḥ* ।	ॐ योगयुक्ताय नमः ।
186.	*Oṃ Bhogayuktāya Namaḥ* ।	ॐ भोगयुक्ताय नमः ।
187.	*Oṃ Śaṅkāmukta Samādhimate Namaḥ* ।	ॐ शङ्कामुक्त समाधिमते नमः ।
188.	*Oṃ Sahajāya Namaḥ* ।	ॐ सहजाय नमः ।
189.	*Oṃ Sakaleśanāya Namaḥ* ।	ॐ सकलेशनाय नमः ।
190.	*Oṃ Kārtavīryavarapradāya Namaḥ* ।	ॐ कार्तवीर्यवरप्रदाय नमः ।
191.	*Oṃ Sarajase Namaḥ* ।	ॐ सरजसे नमः ।
192.	*Oṃ Virajase Namaḥ* ।	ॐ विरजसे नमः ।
193.	*Oṃ Puṃse Namaḥ* ।	ॐ पुंसे नमः ।
194.	*Oṃ Pāvanāya Namaḥ* ।	ॐ पावनाय नमः ।
195.	*Oṃ Pāpanāśanāya Namaḥ* ।	ॐ पापनाशनाय नमः ।
196.	*Oṃ Parāvaravinirmuktāya Namaḥ* ।	ॐ परावरविनिर्मुक्ताय नमः ।
197.	*Oṃ Parañjyotiye Namaḥ* ।	ॐ परञ्ज्योतिये नमः ।
198.	*Oṃ Purātanāya Namaḥ* ।	ॐ पुरातनाय नमः ।
199.	*Oṃ Nānājyotiṣe Namaḥ* ।	ॐ नानाज्योतिषे नमः ।
200.	*Oṃ Anekātmane Namaḥ* ।	ॐ अनेकात्मने नमः ।

201.	*Oṃ Svayañjyotiṣe* |	ॐ स्वयञ्ज्योतिषे ।
202.	*Oṃ Sadāśivāya Namaḥ* |	ॐ सदाशिवाय नमः ।
203.	*Oṃ Divyajyotirmayāya Namaḥ* |	ॐ दिव्यज्योतिर्मयाय नमः ।
204.	*Oṃ Satyavijñānabhāskarāya Namaḥ* |	ॐ सत्यविज्ञानभास्कराय नमः ।
205.	*Oṃ Nityaśuddhāya Namaḥ* |	ॐ नित्यशुद्धाय नमः ।
206.	*Oṃ Parāya Namaḥ* |	ॐ पराय नमः ।
207.	*Oṃ Pūrṇāya Namaḥ* |	ॐ पूर्णाय नमः ।
208.	*Oṃ Prakāśāya Namaḥ* |	ॐ प्रकाशाय नमः ।
209.	*Oṃ Prakaṭodbhavāya Namaḥ* |	ॐ प्रकटोद्भवाय नमः ।
210.	*Oṃ Pramādavigatāya Namaḥ* |	ॐ प्रमादविगताय नमः ।
211.	*Oṃ Pareśāya Namaḥ* |	ॐ परेशाय नमः ।
212.	*Oṃ Paravikramāya Namaḥ* |	ॐ परविक्रमाय नमः ।
213.	*Oṃ Yogine Namaḥ* |	ॐ योगिने नमः ।
214.	*Oṃ Yogāya Namaḥ* |	ॐ योगाय नमः ।
215.	*Oṃ Yogapāya Namaḥ* |	ॐ योगपाय नमः ।
216.	*Oṃ Yogābhyāsaprakāśanāya Namaḥ* |	ॐ योगाभ्यासप्रकाशनाय नमः ।
217.	*Oṃ Yoktre Namaḥ* |	ॐ योक्त्रे नमः ।
218.	*Oṃ Moktre Namaḥ* |	ॐ मोक्त्रे नमः ।
219.	*Oṃ Vidhātre Namaḥ* |	ॐ विधात्रे नमः ।
220.	*Oṃ Trātre Namaḥ* |	ॐ त्रात्रे नमः ।
221.	*Oṃ Pātre Namaḥ* |	ॐ पात्रे नमः ।
222.	*Oṃ Nirāyudhāya Namaḥ* |	ॐ निरायुधाय नमः ।
223.	*Oṃ Nityamuktāya Namaḥ* |	ॐ नित्यमुक्ताय नमः ।
224.	*Oṃ Nityayuktāya Namaḥ* |	ॐ नित्ययुक्ताय नमः ।
225.	*Oṃ Satyāya Namaḥ* |	ॐ सत्याय नमः ।

226.	*Oṃ Satyaparākramāya Namaḥ* |	ॐ सत्यपराक्रमाय नमः ।
227.	*Oṃ Sattvaśuddhikarāya Namaḥ* |	ॐ सत्त्वशुद्धिकराय नमः ।
228.	*Oṃ Sattvāya Namaḥ* |	ॐ सत्त्वाय नमः ।
229.	*Oṃ Sattvabhṛtāṅgataye Namaḥ* |	ॐ सत्त्वभृताङ्गतये नमः
230.	*Oṃ Śrīdharāya Namaḥ* |	ॐ श्रीधराय नमः ।
231.	*Oṃ Śrīvapuṣe Namaḥ* |	ॐ श्रीवपुषे नमः ।
232.	*Oṃ Śrīmate Namaḥ* |	ॐ श्रीमते नमः ।
233.	*Oṃ Śrīnivāsāya Namaḥ* |	ॐ श्रीनिवासाय नमः ।
234.	*Oṃ Amarārcitāya Namaḥ* |	ॐ अमरार्चिताय नमः ।
235.	*Oṃ Śrīnidhaye Namaḥ* |	ॐ श्रीनिधये नमः ।
236.	*Oṃ Śrīpataye Namaḥ* |	ॐ श्रीपतये नमः ।
237.	*Oṃ Śreṣṭhāya Namaḥ* |	ॐ श्रेष्ठाय नमः ।
238.	*Oṃ Śreyaskāya Namaḥ* |	ॐ श्रेयस्काय नमः ।
239.	*Oṃ Caramāśrayāya Namaḥ* |	ॐ चरमाश्रयाय नमः ।
240.	*Oṃ Tyāgine Namaḥ* |	ॐ त्यागिने नमः ।
241.	*Oṃ Tyāgājyasampannāya Namaḥ* |	ॐ त्यागाज्यसम्पन्नाय नमः ।
242.	*Oṃ Tyāgātmane Namaḥ* |	ॐ त्यागात्मने नमः ।
243.	*Oṃ Tyāgavigrahāya Namaḥ* |	ॐ त्यागविग्रहाय नमः ।
244.	*Oṃ Tyāgalakṣaṇasiddhātmane Namaḥ* |	ॐ त्यागलक्षणसिद्धात्मने नमः ।
245.	*Oṃ Tyāgajñāya Namaḥ* |	ॐ त्यागज्ञाय नमः ।
246.	*Oṃ Tyāgakāraṇāya Namaḥ* |	ॐ त्यागकारणाय नमः ।
247.	*Oṃ Bhāgāya Namaḥ* |	ॐ भागाय नमः ।
248.	*Oṃ Bhoktre Namaḥ* |	ॐ भोक्त्रे नमः ।
249.	*Oṃ Bhogyāya Namaḥ* |	ॐ भोग्याय नमः ।
250.	*Oṃ Bhogasādhanakāraṇāya Namaḥ* |	ॐ भोगसाधनकारणाय नमः ।

251.	*Oṃ Bhogine Namaḥ* I	ॐ भोगिने नमः ।
252.	*Oṃ Bhogārthasampannāya Namaḥ*	ॐ भोगार्थसम्पन्नाय नमः
253.	*Oṃ Bhogajñānaprakāśanāya Namaḥ* I	ॐ भोगज्ञानप्रकाशनाय नमः ।
254.	*Oṃ Kevalāya Namaḥ* I	ॐ केवलाय नमः ।
255.	*Oṃ Keśavāya Namaḥ* I	ॐ केशवाय नमः ।
256.	*Oṃ Kṛṣṇāya Namaḥ* I	ॐ कृष्णाय नमः ।
257.	*Oṃ Kaṃvāsase Namaḥ* I	ॐ कंवाससे नमः ।
258.	*Oṃ Kamalālayāya Namaḥ* I	ॐ कमलालयाय नमः ।
259.	*Oṃ Kamalāsanapūjyāya Namaḥ* I	ॐ कमलासनपूज्याय नमः ।
260.	*Oṃ Haraye Namaḥ* I	ॐ हरये नमः ।
261.	*Oṃ Ajñānakhaṇḍanāya Namaḥ* I	ॐ अज्ञानखण्डनाय नमः
262.	*Oṃ Mahātmane Namaḥ* I	ॐ महात्मने नमः ।
263.	*Oṃ Mahadādaye Namaḥ* I	ॐ महदादये नमः ।
264.	*Oṃ Maheśottamavanditā Namaḥ* I	ॐ महेशोत्तमवन्दिता नमः
265.	*Oṃ Manovṛddhivihīnātmane Namaḥ* I	ॐ मनोवृद्धिविहीनात्मने नमः ।
266.	*Oṃ Mānātmane Namaḥ* I	ॐ मानात्मने नमः ।
267.	*Oṃ Mānavādhipāya Namaḥ* I	ॐ मानवाधिपाय नमः ।
268.	*Oṃ Bhuvaneśāya Namaḥ* I	ॐ भुवनेशाय नमः ।
269.	*Oṃ Vibhūtaye Namaḥ* I	ॐ विभूतये नमः ।
270.	*Oṃ Dhṛtaye Namaḥ* I	ॐ धृतये नमः ।
271.	*Oṃ Medhāye Namaḥ* I	ॐ मेधाये नमः ।
272.	*Oṃ Smṛtaye Namaḥ* I	ॐ स्मृतये नमः ।
273.	*Oṃ Dayāye Namaḥ* I	ॐ दयाये नमः ।
274.	*Oṃ Duḥkhadāvānalāya Namaḥ* I	ॐ दुःखदावानलाय नमः
275.	*Oṃ Buddhāya Namaḥ* I	ॐ बुद्धाय नमः ।

276.	*Oṃ Prabuddhāya Namaḥ* ।	ॐ प्रबुद्धाय नमः ।
277.	*Oṃ Parameśvarāya Namaḥ* ।	ॐ परमेश्वराय नमः ।
278.	*Oṃ Kāmaghnāya Namaḥ* ।	ॐ कामघ्नाय नमः ।
279.	*Oṃ Krodhaghnāya Namaḥ* ।	ॐ क्रोधघ्नाय नमः ।
280.	*Oṃ Dambhadarpamadāpahāya Namaḥ* ।	ॐ दम्भदर्पमदापहाय नमः ।
281.	*Oṃ Ajñānatimirāraye Namaḥ* ।	ॐ अज्ञानतिमिरारये नमः।
282.	*Oṃ Bhavāraye Namaḥ* ।	ॐ भवारये नमः ।
283.	*Oṃ Bhuvaneśvarāya Namaḥ* ।	ॐ भुवनेश्वराय नमः ।
284.	*Oṃ Rūpakṛte Namaḥ* ।	ॐ रूपकृते नमः ।
285.	*Oṃ Rūpabhṛte Namaḥ* ।	ॐ रूपभृते नमः ।
286.	*Oṃ Rūpiṇe Namaḥ* ।	ॐ रूपिणे नमः ।
287.	*Oṃ Rūpātmane Namaḥ* ।	ॐ रूपात्मने नमः ।
288.	*Oṃ Rūpakāraṇāya Namaḥ* ।	ॐ रूपकारणाय नमः ।
289.	*Oṃ Rūpajñāya Namaḥ* ।	ॐ रूपज्ञाय नमः ।
290.	*Oṃ Rūpasākṣiṇe Namaḥ* ।	ॐ रूपसाक्षिणे नमः ।
291.	*Oṃ Nāmarūpāya Namaḥ* ।	ॐ नामरूपाय नमः ।
292.	*Oṃ Guṇāntakāya Namaḥ* ।	ॐ गुणान्तकाय नमः ।
293.	*Oṃ Aprameyāya Namaḥ* ।	ॐ अप्रमेयाय नमः ।
294.	*Oṃ Prameyāya Namaḥ* ।	ॐ प्रमेयाय नमः ।
295.	*Oṃ Pramāṇāya Namaḥ* ।	ॐ प्रमाणाय नमः ।
296.	*Oṃ Praṇavāśrayāya Namaḥ* ।	ॐ प्रणवाश्रयाय नमः ।
297.	*Oṃ Pramāṇarahitāya Namaḥ* ।	ॐ प्रमाणरहिताय नमः ।
298.	*Oṃ Acintyāya Namaḥ* ।	ॐ अचिन्त्याय नमः ।
299.	*Oṃ Cetanāvigatāya Namaḥ* ।	ॐ चेतनाविगताय नमः ।
300.	*Oṃ Ajarāya Namaḥ* ।	ॐ अजराय नमः ।
301.	*Oṃ Akṣarāya Namaḥ* ।	ॐ अक्षराय नमः ।

302.	*Oṃ Akṣaramuktāya Namaḥ* ।	ॐ अक्षरमुक्ताय नमः ।
303.	*Oṃ Vijvarāya Namaḥ* ।	ॐ विज्वराय नमः ।
304.	*Oṃ Jvaranāśanāya Namaḥ* ।	ॐ ज्वरनाशनाय नमः ।
305.	*Oṃ Viśiṣṭāya Namaḥ* ।	ॐ विशिष्टाय नमः ।
306.	*Oṃ Vittaśāstriṇe Namaḥ* ।	ॐ वित्तशास्त्रिणे नमः ।
307.	*Oṃ Dṛṣṭāya Namaḥ* ।	ॐ दृष्टाय नमः ।
308.	*Oṃ Dṛṣṭāntavarjitāya Namaḥ* ।	ॐ दृष्टान्तवर्जिताय नमः ।
309.	*Oṃ Guṇeśāya Namaḥ* ।	ॐ गुणेशाय नमः ।
310.	*Oṃ Guṇakāyāya Namaḥ* ।	ॐ गुणकायाय नमः ।
311.	*Oṃ Guṇātmane Namaḥ* ।	ॐ गुणात्मने नमः ।
312.	*Oṃ Guṇabhāvanāya Namaḥ* ।	ॐ गुणभावनाय नमः ।
313.	*Oṃ Anantaguṇasampannāya Namaḥ* ।	ॐ अनन्तगुणसम्पन्नाय नमः ।
314.	*Oṃ Guṇagarbhāya Namaḥ* ।	ॐ गुणगर्भाय नमः ।
315.	*Oṃ Guṇādhipāya Namaḥ* ।	ॐ गुणाधिपाय नमः ।
316.	*Oṃ Guṇeśāya Namaḥ* ।	ॐ गुणेशाय नमः ।
317.	*Oṃ Guṇanāthāya Namaḥ* ।	ॐ गुणनाथाय नमः ।
318.	*Oṃ Guṇātmane Namaḥ* ।	ॐ गुणात्मने नमः ।
319.	*Oṃ Guṇabhāvanāya Namaḥ* ।	ॐ गुणभावनाय नमः ।
320.	*Oṃ Guṇabandhave Namaḥ* ।	ॐ गुणबन्धवे नमः ।
321.	*Oṃ Vivekātmane Namaḥ* ।	ॐ विवेकात्मने नमः ।
322.	*Oṃ Guṇayuktāya Namaḥ* ।	ॐ गुणयुक्ताय नमः ।
323.	*Oṃ Parākramiṇe Namaḥ* ।	ॐ पराक्रमिणे नमः ।
324.	*Oṃ Atarkāya Namaḥ* ।	ॐ अतर्काय नमः ।
325.	*Oṃ Ākṛtave Namaḥ* ।	ॐ आकृतवे नमः ।
326.	*Oṃ Agnaye Namaḥ* ।	ॐ अग्नये नमः ।
327.	*Oṃ Kṛtajñāya Namaḥ* ।	ॐ कृतज्ञाय नमः ।
328.	*Oṃ Saphalāśrayāya Namaḥ* ।	ॐ सफलाश्रयाय नमः ।

329.	*Oṃ Yajñāya Namaḥ* I	ॐ यज्ञाय नमः ।
330.	*Oṃ Yajñaphaladātre Namaḥ* I	ॐ यज्ञफलदात्रे नमः ।
331.	*Oṃ Yajñātmane Namaḥ* I	ॐ यज्ञात्मने नमः ।
332.	*Oṃ Ījanāya Namaḥ* I	ॐ ईजनाय नमः ।
333.	*Oṃ Amarottamāya Namaḥ* I	ॐ अमरोत्तमाय नमः ।
334.	*Oṃ Hiraṇyagarbhāya Namaḥ* I	ॐ हिरण्यगर्भाय नमः ।
335.	*Oṃ Śrīgarbhāya Namaḥ* I	ॐ श्रीगर्भाय नमः ।
336.	*Oṃ Svagarbhāya Namaḥ* I	ॐ स्वगर्भाय नमः ।
337.	*Oṃ Kuṇapeśvarāya Namaḥ* I	ॐ कुणपेश्वराय नमः ।
338.	*Oṃ Māyogarbhāya Namaḥ* I	ॐ मायोगर्भाय नमः ।
339.	*Oṃ Lokagarbhāya Namaḥ* I	ॐ लोकगर्भाय नमः ।
340.	*Oṃ Svayambhuve Namaḥ* I	ॐ स्वयम्भुवे नमः ।
341.	*Oṃ Bhuvanāntakāya Namaḥ* I	ॐ भुवनान्तकाय नमः ।
342.	*Oṃ Niṣpāpāya Namaḥ* I	ॐ निष्पापाय नमः ।
343.	*Oṃ Nibiḍāya Namaḥ* I	ॐ निबिडाय नमः ।
344.	*Oṃ Nandine Namaḥ* I	ॐ नन्दिने नमः ।
345.	*Oṃ Bodhine Namaḥ* I	ॐ बोधिने नमः ।
346.	*Oṃ Bodhasamāśrayāya Namaḥ* I	ॐ बोधसमाश्रयाय नमः ।
347.	*Oṃ Bodhātmane Namaḥ* I	ॐ बोधात्मने नमः ।
348.	*Oṃ Bodhanātmane Namaḥ* I	ॐ बोधनात्मने नमः ।
349.	*Oṃ Bhedavaitaṇḍakhaṇḍanāya Namaḥ* I	ॐ भेदवैतण्डखण्डनाय नमः ।
350.	*Oṃ Svabhāvyāya Namaḥ* I	ॐ स्वभाव्याय नमः ।
351.	*Oṃ Bhāvavimuktāya Namaḥ* I	ॐ भावविमुक्ताय नमः ।
352.	*Oṃ Vyaktāya Namaḥ* I	ॐ व्यक्ताय नमः ।
353.	*Oṃ Avyaktasamāśrayāya Namaḥ* I	ॐ अव्यक्तसमाश्रयाय नमः ।
354.	*Oṃ Nityatṛptāya Namaḥ* I	ॐ नित्यतृप्ताय नमः ।

355.	*Oṃ Nirābhāsāya Namaḥ* |	ॐ निराभासाय नमः।
356.	*Oṃ Nirvāṇāya Namaḥ* |	ॐ निर्वाणाय नमः।
357.	*Oṃ Śaraṇāya Namaḥ* |	ॐ शरणाय नमः।
358.	*Oṃ Suhṛde Namaḥ* |	ॐ सुहृदे नमः।
359.	*Oṃ Guhyeśāya Namaḥ* |	ॐ गुह्येशाय नमः।
360.	*Oṃ Guṇagambhīrāya Namaḥ* |	ॐ गुणगम्भीराय नमः।
361.	*Oṃ Guṇadeśanivāraṇāya Namaḥ* |	ॐ गुणदेशनिवारणाय नमः।
362.	*Oṃ Guṇasaṅgavihīnāya Namaḥ* |	ॐ गुणसङ्गविहीनाय नमः।
363.	*Oṃ Yogārerdarpanāśanāya Namaḥ* |	ॐ योगारेर्दर्पनाशनाय नमः।
364.	*Oṃ Ānandāya Namaḥ* |	ॐ आनन्दाय नमः।
365.	*Oṃ Paramānandāya Namaḥ* |	ॐ परमानन्दाय नमः।
366.	*Oṃ Svānandasukhavardhanāya Namaḥ* |	ॐ स्वानन्दसुखवर्धनाय नमः।
367.	*Oṃ Satyānandāya Namaḥ* |	ॐ सत्यानन्दाय नमः।
368.	*Oṃ Cidānandāya Namaḥ* |	ॐ चिदानन्दाय नमः।
369.	*Oṃ Sarvānandaparāyaṇāya Namaḥ* |	ॐ सर्वानन्दपरायणाय नमः।
370.	*Oṃ Sadrūpāya Namaḥ* |	ॐ सद्रूपाय नमः।
371.	*Oṃ Sahajāya Namaḥ* |	ॐ सहजाय नमः।
372.	*Oṃ Satyāya Namaḥ* |	ॐ सत्याय नमः।
373.	*Oṃ Svānandāya Namaḥ* |	ॐ स्वानन्दाय नमः।
374.	*Oṃ Sumanoharāya Namaḥ* |	ॐ सुमनोहराय नमः।
375.	*Oṃ Sarvāya Namaḥ* |	ॐ सर्वाय नमः।
376.	*Oṃ Sarvāntarāya Namaḥ* |	ॐ सर्वान्तराय नमः।
377.	*Oṃ Pūrvātpūrvāntarāya Namaḥ* |	ॐ पूर्वात्पूर्वान्तराय नमः।
378.	*Oṃ Svamayāya Namaḥ* |	ॐ स्वमयाय नमः।

379.	*Oṃ Svaparāya Namaḥ* ।	ॐ स्वपराय नमः ।
380.	*Oṃ Svādaye Namaḥ* ।	ॐ स्वादये नमः ।
381.	*Oṃ Svambrahmaṇe Namaḥ* ।	ॐ स्वम्ब्रह्मणे नमः ।
382.	*Oṃ Svatanave Namaḥ* ।	ॐ स्वतनवे नमः ।
383.	*Oṃ Svagāya Namaḥ* ।	ॐ स्वगाय नमः ।
384.	*Oṃ Svavāsase Namaḥ* ।	ॐ स्ववाससे नमः ।
385.	*Oṃ Svavihīnāya Namaḥ* ।	ॐ स्वविहीनाय नमः ।
386.	*Oṃ Svanidhaye Namaḥ* ।	ॐ स्वनिधये नमः ।
387.	*Oṃ Svaparākṣayāya Namaḥ* ।	ॐ स्वपराक्षयाय नमः ।
388.	*Oṃ Anantāya Namaḥ* ।	ॐ अनन्ताय नमः ।
389.	*Oṃ Ādirūpāya Namaḥ* ।	ॐ आदिरूपाय नमः ।
390.	*Oṃ Sūryamaṇḍalamadhyagāya Namaḥ* ।	ॐ सूर्यमण्डलमध्यगाय नमः ।
391.	*Oṃ Amoghāya Namaḥ* ।	ॐ अमोघाय नमः ।
392.	*Oṃ Paramāmoghāya Namaḥ* ।	ॐ परमामोघाय नमः ।
393.	*Oṃ Pareśāya Namaḥ* ।	ॐ परेशाय नमः ।
394.	*Oṃ Parādāya Namaḥ* ।	ॐ परादाय नमः ।
395.	*Oṃ Kavaye Namaḥ* ।	ॐ कवये नमः ।
396.	*Oṃ Viśvacakṣuṣe Namaḥ* ।	ॐ विश्वचक्षुषे नमः ।
397.	*Oṃ Viśvasākṣiṇe Namaḥ* ।	ॐ विश्वसाक्षिणे नमः ।
398.	*Oṃ Viśvabāhave Namaḥ* ।	ॐ विश्वबाहवे नमः ।
399.	*Oṃ Dhaneśvarāya Namaḥ* ।	ॐ धनेश्वराय नमः ।
400.	*Oṃ Dhanañjayāya Namaḥ* ।	ॐ धनञ्जयाय नमः ।
401.	*Oṃ Mahātejase Namaḥ* ।	ॐ महातेजसे नमः ।
402.	*Oṃ Tejiṣṭhāya Namaḥ* ।	ॐ तेजिष्ठाय नमः ।
403.	*Oṃ Tejasāya Namaḥ* ।	ॐ तेजसाय नमः ।
404.	*Oṃ Sukhine Namaḥ* ।	ॐ सुखिने नमः ।
405.	*Oṃ Jyotiṣe Namaḥ* ।	ॐ ज्योतिषे नमः ।

406.	*Oṃ Jyotirmayāya Namaḥ* |	ॐ ज्योतिर्मयाय नमः ।
407.	*Oṃ Jetre Namaḥ* |	ॐ जेत्रे नमः ।
408.	*Oṃ Jyotiṣāṃ Jyotirātmakāya Namaḥ* |	ॐ ज्योतिषां ज्योति रात्मकाय नमः ।
409.	*Oṃ Jyotiṣāmapi Jyotiṣe Namaḥ* |	ॐ ज्योतिषामपि ज्योतिषे नमः ।
410.	*Oṃ Janakāya Namaḥ* |	ॐ जनकाय नमः ।
411.	*Oṃ Janamohanāya Namaḥ* |	ॐ जनमोहनाय नमः ।
412.	*Oṃ Jitendriyāya Namaḥ* |	ॐ जितेन्द्रियाय नमः ।
413.	*Oṃ Jitakrodhāya Namaḥ* |	ॐ जितक्रोधाय नमः ।
414.	*Oṃ Jitātmane Namaḥ* |	ॐ जितात्मने नमः ।
415.	*Oṃ Jitamānasāya Namaḥ* |	ॐ जितमानसाय नमः ।
416.	*Oṃ Jitasaṅgāya Namaḥ* |	ॐ जितसङ्गाय नमः ।
417.	*Oṃ Jitaprāṇāya Namaḥ* |	ॐ जितप्राणाय नमः ।
418.	*Oṃ Jitasaṃsāra Namaḥ* |	ॐ जितसंसार नमः ।
419.	*Oṃ Nirvāsanāya Namaḥ* |	ॐ निर्वासनाय नमः ।
420.	*Oṃ Nirālambāya Namaḥ* |	ॐ निरालम्बाय नमः ।
421.	*Oṃ Niryogakṣemavarjitāya Namaḥ* |	ॐ निर्योगक्षेमवर्जिताय नमः ।
422.	*Oṃ Nirīhāya Namaḥ* |	ॐ निरीहाय नमः ।
423.	*Oṃ Nirahaṅkārāya Namaḥ* |	ॐ निरहङ्काराय नमः ।
424.	*Oṃ Nirāśīnirupādhikāya Namaḥ* |	ॐ निराशीनिरुपाधिकाय नमः ।
425.	*Oṃ Nirlābodhyāya Namaḥ* |	ॐ निर्लाबोध्याय नमः ।
426.	*Oṃ Viviktātmane Namaḥ* |	ॐ विविक्तात्मने नमः ।
427.	*Oṃ Viśuddhottama Gauravāya Namaḥ* |	ॐ विशुद्धोत्तम गौरवाय नमः ।
428.	*Oṃ Vidyāyine Namaḥ* |	ॐ विद्यायिने नमः ।
429.	*Oṃ Paramārthine Namaḥ* |	ॐ परमार्थिने नमः ।

430.	*Oṃ Śraddhārthine Namaḥ* ।	ॐ श्रद्धार्थिने नमः ।
431.	*Oṃ Sādhanātmakāya Namaḥ* ।	ॐ साधनात्मकाय नमः ।
432.	*Oṃ Pratyāhāriṇe Namaḥ* ।	ॐ प्रत्याहारिणे नमः ।
433.	*Oṃ Nirāhāriṇe Namaḥ* ।	ॐ निराहारिणे नमः ।
434.	*Oṃ Sarvāhāraparāyaṇāya Namaḥ* ।	ॐ सर्वाहारपरायणाय नमः ।
435.	*Oṃ Nityaśuddhāya Namaḥ* ।	ॐ नित्यशुद्धाय नमः ।
436.	*Oṃ Nirākāṅkṣiṇe Namaḥ* ।	ॐ निराकाङ्क्षिणे नमः ।
437.	*Oṃ Pārāyaṇaparāyaṇāya Namaḥ* ।	ॐ पारायणपरायणाय नमः ।
438.	*Oṃ Aṇornutarayā Namaḥ* ।	ॐ अणोर्नुतरया नमः ।
439.	*Oṃ Sūkṣmāya Namaḥ* ।	ॐ सूक्ष्माय नमः ।
440.	*Oṃ Sthūlāya Namaḥ* ।	ॐ स्थूलाय नमः ।
441.	*Oṃ Sthūlatarāya Namaḥ* ।	ॐ स्थूलतराय नमः ।
442.	*Oṃ Ekāya Namaḥ* ।	ॐ एकाय नमः ।
443.	*Oṃ Anekarūpāya Namaḥ* ।	ॐ अनेकरूपाय नमः ।
444.	*Oṃ Viśvarūpāya Namaḥ* ।	ॐ विश्वरूपाय नमः ।
445.	*Oṃ Sanātanāya Namaḥ* ।	ॐ सनातनाय नमः ।
446.	*Oṃ Naikarūpāya Namaḥ* ।	ॐ नैकरूपाय नमः ।
447.	*Oṃ Nirūpātmane Namaḥ* ।	ॐ निरूपात्मने नमः ।
448.	*Oṃ Naikabodhamayāya Namaḥ* ।	ॐ नैकबोधमयाय नमः ।
449.	*Oṃ Naikanāmamayāya Namaḥ* ।	ॐ नैकनाममयाय नमः ।
450.	*Oṃ Naikavidyāvivardhanāya Namaḥ* ।	ॐ नैकविद्याविवर्धनाय नमः ।
451.	*Oṃ Ekāya Namaḥ* ।	ॐ एकाय नमः ।
452.	*Oṃ Ekāntikāya Namaḥ* ।	ॐ एकान्तिकाय नमः ।
453.	*Oṃ Nānābhāvavivarjitāya Namaḥ* ।	ॐ नानाभाववविवर्जिताय नमः ।

454.	*Oṃ Ekākṣarāya Namaḥ* ।	ॐ एकाक्षराय नमः ।
455.	*Oṃ Bījāya Namaḥ* ।	ॐ बीजाय नमः ।
456.	*Oṃ Pūrṇabimbāya Namaḥ* ।	ॐ पूर्णबिम्बाय नमः ।
457.	*Oṃ Sanātanāya Namaḥ* ।	ॐ सनातनाय नमः ।
458.	*Oṃ Mantravīryāya Namaḥ* ।	ॐ मन्त्रवीर्याय नमः ।
459.	*Oṃ Mantrabījāya Namaḥ* ।	ॐ मन्त्रबीजाय नमः ।
460.	*Oṃ Śāstravīryāya Namaḥ* ।	ॐ शास्त्रवीर्याय नमः ।
461.	*Oṃ Jagatpataye Namaḥ* ।	ॐ जगत्पतये नमः ।
462.	*Oṃ Nānāvīryadharāya Namaḥ* ।	ॐ नानावीर्यधराय नमः ।
463.	*Oṃ Śaktreśāya Namaḥ* ।	ॐ शक्त्रेशाय नमः ।
464.	*Oṃ Pṛthivīpataye Namaḥ* ।	ॐ पृथिवीपतये नमः ।
465.	*Oṃ Prāṇeśāya Namaḥ* ।	ॐ प्राणेशाय नमः ।
466.	*Oṃ Prāṇadāya Namaḥ* ।	ॐ प्राणदाय नमः ।
467.	*Oṃ Prāṇāya Namaḥ* ।	ॐ प्राणाय नमः ।
468.	*Oṃ Prāṇāyāmaparāyaṇāya Namaḥ* ।	ॐ प्राणायामपरायणाय नमः ।
469.	*Oṃ Praṇapañcakanirmuktāya Namaḥ* ।	ॐ प्रणपञ्चकनिर्मुक्ताय नमः ।
470.	*Oṃ Kośapañcakavarjitāya Namaḥ* ।	ॐ कोशपञ्चकवर्जिताय नमः ।
471.	*Oṃ Niścalāya Namaḥ* ।	ॐ निश्चलाय नमः ।
472.	*Oṃ Niṣkalāya Namaḥ* ।	ॐ निष्कलाय नमः ।
473.	*Oṃ Āṅgāya Namaḥ* ।	ॐ आङ्गाय नमः ।
474.	*Oṃ Niṣprapañcāya Namaḥ* ।	ॐ निष्प्रपञ्चाय नमः ।
475.	*Oṃ Nirāmayāya Namaḥ* ।	ॐ निरामयाय नमः ।
476.	*Oṃ Nirādhārāya Namaḥ* ।	ॐ निराधाराय नमः ।
477.	*Oṃ Nirākārāya Namaḥ* ।	ॐ निराकाराय नमः ।
478.	*Oṃ Nirvikāryāya Namaḥ* ।	ॐ निर्विकार्याय नमः ।

479.	*Oṃ Nirañjanāya Namaḥ* |	ॐ निरञ्जनाय नमः ।
480.	*Oṃ Niṣpratītāya Namaḥ* |	ॐ निष्प्रतीताय नमः ।
481.	*Oṃ Nirābhāsāya Namaḥ* |	ॐ निराभासाय नमः ।
482.	*Oṃ Nirāsaktāya Namaḥ* |	ॐ निरासक्ताय नमः ।
483.	*Oṃ Nirākulāya Namaḥ* |	ॐ निराकुलाय नमः ।
484.	*Oṃ Niṣṭhāsarvagatāya Namaḥ* |	ॐ निष्ठासर्वगताय नमः ।
485.	*Oṃ Nirārambhāya Namaḥ* |	ॐ निरारम्भाय नमः ।
486.	*Oṃ Nirāśrayāya Namaḥ* |	ॐ निराश्रयाय नमः ।
487.	*Oṃ Nirantarāya Namaḥ* |	ॐ निरन्तराय नमः ।
488.	*Oṃ Sattvagoptre Namaḥ* |	ॐ सत्त्वगोप्त्रे नमः ।
489.	*Oṃ Śāntāya Namaḥ* |	ॐ शान्ताय नमः ।
490.	*Oṃ Dāntāya Namaḥ* |	ॐ दान्ताय नमः ।
491.	*Oṃ Mahāmunaye Namaḥ* |	ॐ महामुनये नमः ।
492.	*Oṃ Niḥśabdāya Namaḥ* |	ॐ निःशब्दाय नमः ।
493.	*Oṃ Sukṛtāya Namaḥ* |	ॐ सुकृताय नमः ।
494.	*Oṃ Svasthāya Namaḥ* |	ॐ स्वस्थाय नमः ।
495.	*Oṃ Satyavādine Namaḥ* |	ॐ सत्यवादिने नमः ।
496.	*Oṃ Sureśvarāya Namaḥ* |	ॐ सुरेश्वराय नमः ।
497.	*Oṃ Jñānadāya Namaḥ* |	ॐ ज्ञानदाय नमः ।
498.	*Oṃ Jñānavijñānine Namaḥ* |	ॐ ज्ञानविज्ञानिने नमः ।
499.	*Oṃ Jñānātmane Namaḥ* |	ॐ ज्ञानात्मने नमः ।
500.	*Oṃ Ānandapūretāya Namaḥ* |	ॐ आनन्दपूरेताय नमः ।
501.	*Oṃ Jñānayajñavidāṃ Dakṣāya Namaḥ* |	ॐ ज्ञानयज्ञविदां दक्षाय नमः ।
502.	*Oṃ Jñānāgnaye Namaḥ* |	ॐ ज्ञानाग्नये नमः ।
503.	*Oṃ Jvalanāya Namaḥ* |	ॐ ज्वलनाय नमः ।
504.	*Oṃ Budhāya Namaḥ* |	ॐ बुधाय नमः ।

505.	*Oṃ Dayāvate Namaḥ* |	ॐ दयावते नमः ।
506.	*Oṃ Bhavarogāraye Namaḥ* |	ॐ भवरोगारये नमः ।
507.	*Oṃ Cikitsā Caramāgalāye Namaḥ* |	ॐ चिकित्सा चरमा गलाये नमः ।
508.	*Oṃ Candramaṇḍala Madhyasthāya Namaḥ* |	ॐ चन्द्रमण्डल मध्यस्थाय नमः ।
509.	*Oṃ Candrakoṭisuśīlālaye Namaḥ* |	ॐ चन्द्रकोटिसुशीलालये नमः ।
510.	*Oṃ Yantrakṛte Namaḥ* |	ॐ यन्त्रकृते नमः ।
511.	*Oṃ Paramāya Namaḥ* |	ॐ परमाय नमः ।
512.	*Oṃ Yantriṇe Namaḥ* |	ॐ यन्त्रिणे नमः ।
513.	*Oṃ Yantrārūḍhāparājitāya Namaḥ* |	ॐ यन्त्रारूढापराजिताय नमः ।
514.	*Oṃ Yantravide Namaḥ* |	ॐ यन्त्रविदे नमः ।
515.	*Oṃ Yantravāsāya Namaḥ* |	ॐ यन्त्रवासाय नमः ।
516.	*Oṃ Yantrādhārāya Namaḥ* |	ॐ यन्त्राधाराय नमः ।
517.	*Oṃ Dharādhārāya Namaḥ* |	ॐ धराधाराय नमः ।
518.	*Oṃ Tattvajñāya Namaḥ* |	ॐ तत्त्वज्ञाय नमः ।
519.	*Oṃ Tattvabhūtātmane Namaḥ* |	ॐ तत्त्वभूतात्मने नमः ।
520.	*Oṃ Mahattattvaprakāśanāya Namaḥ* |	ॐ महत्तत्त्वप्रकाशनाय नमः ।
521.	*Oṃ Tattvasaṅkhyānayogajñāya Namaḥ* |	ॐ तत्त्व सङ्ख्यान योगज्ञाय नमः ।
522.	*Oṃ Sāṅkhyaśāstrapravartakāya Namaḥ* |	ॐ साङ्ख्य शास्त्र प्रवर्तकाय नमः ।
523.	*Oṃ Ananta Vikramāya Namaḥ* |	ॐ अनन्त विक्रमाय नमः ।
524.	*Oṃ Devāya Namaḥ* |	ॐ देवाय नमः ।
525.	*Oṃ Mādhavāya Namaḥ* |	ॐ माधवाय नमः ।

526.	*Oṃ Dhaneśvarāya Namaḥ* I	ॐ धनेश्वराय नमः ।
527.	*Oṃ Sādhave Namaḥ* I	ॐ साधवे नमः ।
528.	*Oṃ Sādhu Variṣṭhātmane Namaḥ* I	ॐ साधु वरिष्ठात्मने नमः।
529.	*Oṃ Sāvadhānāya Namaḥ* I	ॐ सावधानाय नमः ।
530.	*Oṃ Amarottamāya Namaḥ* I	ॐ अमरोत्तमाय नमः ।
531.	*Oṃ Niḥsaṅkalpāya Namaḥ* I	ॐ निःसङ्कल्पाय नमः ।
532.	*Oṃ Nirādhārāya Namaḥ* I	ॐ निराधाराय नमः ।
533.	*Oṃ Durdharāya Namaḥ* I	ॐ दुर्धराय नमः ।
534.	*Oṃ Ātmavide Namaḥ* I	ॐ आत्मविदे नमः ।
535.	*Oṃ Pataye Namaḥ* I	ॐ पतये नमः ।
536.	*Oṃ Ārogyasukhadāya Namaḥ* I	ॐ आरोग्यसुखदाय नमः।
537.	*Oṃ Pravarāya Namaḥ* I	ॐ प्रवराय नमः ।
538.	*Oṃ Vāsavāya Namaḥ* I	ॐ वासवाय नमः ।
539.	*Oṃ Pareśāya Namaḥ* I	ॐ परेशाय नमः ।
540.	*Oṃ Paramodārāya Namaḥ* I	ॐ परमोदाराय नमः ।
541.	*Oṃ Pratyakcaitanya Durgamāya Namaḥ* I	ॐ प्रत्यक्चैतन्य दुर्गमाय नमः ।
542.	*Oṃ Durādharṣāya Namaḥ* I	ॐ दुराधर्षाय नमः ।
543.	*Oṃ Durāvāsāya Namaḥ* I	ॐ दुरावासाय नमः ।
544.	*Oṃ Dūratvaparināśanāya Namaḥ* I	ॐ दूरत्वपरिनाशनाय नमः ।
545.	*Oṃ Vedavide Namaḥ* I	ॐ वेदविदे नमः ।
546.	*Oṃ Vedakṛte Namaḥ* I	ॐ वेदकृते नमः ।
547.	*Oṃ Vedāya Namaḥ* I	ॐ वेदाय नमः ।
548.	*Oṃ Vedātmane Namaḥ* I	ॐ वेदात्मने नमः ।
549.	*Oṃ Vimalāśayāya Namaḥ* I	ॐ विमलाशयाय नमः ।
550.	*Oṃ Viviktasevine Namaḥ* I	ॐ विविक्तसेविने नमः ।

551.	*Oṃ Saṃsāraśramanāśanāya Namaḥ* |	ॐ संसारश्रमनाशनाय नमः ।
552.	*Oṃ Brahmayonaye Namaḥ* |	ॐ ब्रह्मयोनये नमः ।
553.	*Oṃ Bṛhadyonaye Namaḥ* |	ॐ बृहद्योनये नमः ।
554.	*Oṃ Viśvayonaye Namaḥ* |	ॐ विश्वयोनये नमः ।
555.	*Oṃ Videhavate Namaḥ* |	ॐ विदेहवते नमः ।
556.	*Oṃ Viśālākṣāya Namaḥ* |	ॐ विशालाक्षाय नमः ।
557.	*Oṃ Viśvanāthāya Namaḥ* |	ॐ विश्वनाथाय नमः ।
558.	*Oṃ Hāṭakāṅgadabhūṣaṇāya Namaḥ* |	ॐ हाटकाङ्गदभूषणाय नमः ।
559.	*Oṃ Abādhyāya Namaḥ* |	ॐ अबाध्याय नमः ।
560.	*Oṃ Jagadārādhyāya Namaḥ* |	ॐ जगदाराध्याय नमः ।
561.	*Oṃ Jagadākhilapālanāya Namaḥ* |	ॐ जगदाखिलपालनाय नमः ।
562.	*Oṃ Janavate Namaḥ* |	ॐ जनवते नमः ।
563.	*Oṃ Dhanavate Namaḥ* |	ॐ धनवते नमः ।
564.	*Oṃ Dharmiṇe Namaḥ* |	ॐ धर्मिणे नमः ।
565.	*Oṃ Dharmagāya Namaḥ* |	ॐ धर्मगाय नमः ।
566.	*Oṃ Dharmavardhanāya Namaḥ* |	ॐ धर्मवर्धनाय नमः ।
567.	*Oṃ Amṛtāya Namaḥ* |	ॐ अमृताय नमः ।
568.	*Oṃ Śāśvatāya Namaḥ* |	ॐ शाश्वताय नमः ।
569.	*Oṃ Sādhyāya Namaḥ* |	ॐ साध्याय नमः ।
570.	*Oṃ Siddhidāya Namaḥ* |	ॐ सिद्धिदाय नमः ।
571.	*Oṃ Sumanoharāya Namaḥ* |	ॐ सुमनोहराय नमः ।
572.	*Oṃ Khalubrahma Khalusthānāya Namaḥ* |	ॐ खलुब्रह्म खलुस्थानाय नमः ।
573.	*Oṃ Munīnāṃ Paramāgataye Namaḥ* |	ॐ मुनीनां परमागतये नमः ।
574.	*Oṃ Upadṛṣṭe Namaḥ* |	ॐ उपदृष्टे नमः ।

575.	*Oṃ Śreṣṭhāya Namaḥ* |	ॐ श्रेष्ठाय नमः ।
576.	*Oṃ Śucirbhūtāya Namaḥ* |	ॐ शुचिर्भूताय नमः ।
577.	*Oṃ Anāmayāya Namaḥ* |	ॐ अनामयाय नमः ।
578.	*Oṃ Vedasiddhāntavedyāya Namaḥ* |	ॐ वेदसिद्धान्तवेद्याय नमः ।
579.	*Oṃ Mānasāhlādavardhanāya Namaḥ* |	ॐ मानसाह्लादवर्धनाय नमः ।
580.	*Oṃ Dehādanyāya Namaḥ* |	ॐ देहादन्याय नमः ।
581.	*Oṃ Guṇādanyāya Namaḥ* |	ॐ गुणादन्याय नमः ।
582.	*Oṃ Lokādanyāya Namaḥ* |	ॐ लोकादन्याय नमः ।
583.	*Oṃ Vivekavide Namaḥ* |	ॐ विवेकविदे नमः ।
584.	*Oṃ Duṣṭasvapnaharāya Namaḥ* |	ॐ दुष्टस्वप्नहराय नमः ।
585.	*Oṃ Gurave Namaḥ* |	ॐ गुरवे नमः ।
586.	*Oṃ Guruvarottamāya Namaḥ* |	ॐ गुरुवरोत्तमाय नमः ।
587.	*Oṃ Karmiṇe Namaḥ* |	ॐ कर्मिणे नमः ।
588.	*Oṃ Karmavinirmuktāya Namaḥ* |	ॐ कर्मविनिर्मुक्ताय नमः ।
589.	*Oṃ Saṃnyāsine Namaḥ* |	ॐ संन्यासिने नमः ।
590.	*Oṃ Sādhakeśvarāya Namaḥ* |	ॐ साधकेश्वराय नमः ।
591.	*Oṃ Sarvabhāvavihināya Namaḥ* |	ॐ सर्वभावविहिनाय नमः
592.	*Oṃ Tṛṣṇāsaṅganivāraṇāya Namaḥ* |	ॐ तृष्णासङ्गनिवारणाय नमः ।
593.	*Oṃ Tyāgine Namaḥ* |	ॐ त्यागिने नमः ।
594.	*Oṃ Tyagavapuṣe Namaḥ* |	ॐ त्यगवपुषे नमः ।
595.	*Oṃ Tyāgāya Namaḥ* |	ॐ त्यागाय नमः ।
596.	*Oṃ Tyāgadānavivarjitāya Namaḥ* |	ॐ त्यागदानविवर्जिताय नमः ।
597.	*Oṃ Tyāgakāraṇatyāgātmane Namaḥ* |	ॐ त्यागकारणत्यागात्मने नमः ।
598.	*Oṃ Sadgurave Namaḥ* |	ॐ सद्गुरवे नमः

599.	*Oṃ Sukhadāyakāya Namaḥ* |	ॐ सुखदायकाय नमः ।
600.	*Oṃ Dakṣāya Namaḥ* |	ॐ दक्षाय नमः ।
601.	*Oṃ Dakṣādi Vandyāya Namaḥ* |	ॐ दक्षादि वन्द्याय नमः ।
602.	*Oṃ Jñānavādapravatakāya Namaḥ* |	ॐ ज्ञानवादप्रवतकाय नमः ।
603.	*Oṃ Śabdabrahmamayātmane Namaḥ* |	ॐ शब्दब्रह्ममयात्मने नमः ।
604.	*Oṃ Śabdabrahmaprakāśavate Namaḥ* |	ॐ शब्दब्रह्मप्रकाशवते नमः ।
605.	*Oṃ Grasiṣṇave Namaḥ* |	ॐ ग्रसिष्णवे नमः ।
606.	*Oṃ Prabhaviṣṇave Namaḥ* |	ॐ प्रभविष्णवे नमः ।
607.	*Oṃ Sahiṣṇave Namaḥ* |	ॐ सहिष्णवे नमः ।
608.	*Oṃ Vigatāntarāya Namaḥ* |	ॐ विगतान्तराय नमः ।
609.	*Oṃ Vidvattamāya Namaḥ* |	ॐ विद्वत्तमाय नमः ।
610.	*Oṃ Mahāvandyāya Namaḥ* |	ॐ महावन्द्याय नमः ।
611.	*Oṃ Viśālottama Vāṅmunaye Namaḥ* |	ॐ विशालोत्तम वाङ्मुनये नमः ।
612.	*Oṃ Brahmavide Namaḥ* |	ॐ ब्रह्मविदे नमः ।
613.	*Oṃ Brahmabhāvāya Namaḥ* |	ॐ ब्रह्मभावाय नमः ।
614.	*Oṃ Brahmarṣaye Namaḥ* |	ॐ ब्रह्मऋषये नमः ।
615.	*Oṃ Brāhmaṇapriyāya Namaḥ* |	ॐ ब्राह्मणप्रियाय नमः ।
616.	*Oṃ Brahmaṇe Namaḥ* |	ॐ ब्रह्मणे नमः ।
617.	*Oṃ Brahmaprakāśātmane Namaḥ* |	ॐ ब्रह्मप्रकाशात्मने नमः।
618.	*Oṃ Brahmavidyāprakāśanāya Namaḥ* |	ॐ ब्रह्मविद्याप्रकाशनाय नमः ।
619.	*Oṃ Atrivaṃśaprabhūtātmane Namaḥ* |	ॐ अत्रिवंशप्रभूतात्मने नमः ।
620.	*Oṃ Tāpasottam Vanditāya Namaḥ* |	ॐ तापसोत्तम् वन्दिताय नमः ।

621.	*Oṃ Ātmavāsine Namaḥ* I	ॐ आत्मवासिने नमः ।
622.	*Oṃ Vidheyātmane Namaḥ* I	ॐ विधेयात्मने नमः ।
623.	*Oṃ Atrivaṃśavivardhanāya Namaḥ* I	ॐ अत्रिवंशविवर्धनाय नमः ।
624.	*Oṃ Pravartanāya Namaḥ* I	ॐ प्रवर्तनाय नमः ।
625.	*Oṃ Nivṛttātmane Namaḥ* I	ॐ निवृत्तात्मने नमः ।
626.	*Oṃ Pralayodakasannibhāya Namaḥ* I	ॐ प्रलयोदकसन्निभाय नमः ।
627.	*Oṃ Nārāyaṇāya Namaḥ* I	ॐ नारायणाय नमः ।
628.	*Oṃ Mahāgarbhāya Namaḥ* I	ॐ महागर्भाय नमः ।
629.	*Oṃ Bhārgavapriyakṛttamāya Namaḥ* I	ॐ भार्गवप्रियकृत्तमाय नमः ।
630.	*Oṃ Saṅkalpaduḥkhadalanāya Namaḥ* I	ॐ सङ्कल्पदुःखदलनाय नमः ।
631.	*Oṃ Saṃsāratamanāśanāya Namaḥ* I	ॐ संसारतमनाशनाय नमः ।
632.	*Oṃ Trivikramāya Namaḥ* I	ॐ त्रिविक्रमाय नमः ।
633.	*Oṃ Tridhākārāya Namaḥ* I	ॐ त्रिधाकाराय नमः ।
634.	*Oṃ Trimūrtaye Namaḥ* I	ॐ त्रिमूर्तये नमः ।
635.	*Oṃ Triguṇātmakāya Namaḥ* I	ॐ त्रिगुणात्मकाय नमः ।
636.	*Oṃ Bhedatrayaharāya Namaḥ* I	ॐ भेदत्रयहराय नमः ।
637.	*Oṃ Tāpatrayanivārakāya Namaḥ* I	ॐ तापत्रयनिवारकाय नमः ।
638.	*Oṃ Doṣatrayavibhedine Namaḥ* I	ॐ दोषत्रयविभेदिने नमः ।
639.	*Oṃ Saṃśayārṇavakhaṇḍanāya Namaḥ* I	ॐ संशयार्णवखण्डनाय नमः ।
640.	*Oṃ Asaṃśayāya Namaḥ* I	ॐ असंशयाय नमः ।
641.	*Oṃ Asaṃmūḍhāya Namaḥ* I	ॐ असंमूढाय नमः ।
642.	*Oṃ Avādine Namaḥ* I	ॐ अवादिने नमः ।

643.	*Oṃ Rājavanditāya Namaḥ* |	ॐ राजवन्दिताय नमः ।
644.	*Oṃ Rājayogine Namaḥ* |	ॐ राजयोगिने नमः ।
645.	*Oṃ Mahāyogine Namaḥ* |	ॐ महायोगिने नमः ।
646.	*Oṃ Svabhāvagalitāya Namaḥ* |	ॐ स्वभावगलिताय नमः।
647.	*Oṃ Puṇyaślokāya Namaḥ* |	ॐ पुण्यश्लोकाय नमः ।
648.	*Oṃ Pavitrāṅghraye Namaḥ* |	ॐ पवित्राङ्घ्रये नमः ।
649.	*Oṃ Dhyānayogaparāyaṇāya Namaḥ* |	ॐ ध्यानयोगपरायणाय नमः ।
650.	*Oṃ Dhyānasthāya Namaḥ* |	ॐ ध्यानस्थाय नमः ।
651.	*Oṃ Dhyānagamyāya Namaḥ* |	ॐ ध्यानगम्याय नमः ।
652.	*Oṃ Vidheyātmane Namaḥ* |	ॐ विधेयात्मने नमः ।
653.	*Oṃ Purātanāya Namaḥ* |	ॐ पुरातनाय नमः ।
654.	*Oṃ Avijñeyāya Namaḥ* |	ॐ अविज्ञेयाय नमः ।
655.	*Oṃ Antarātmane Namaḥ* |	ॐ अन्तरात्मने नमः ।
656.	*Oṃ Mukhyabimbasanātanāya Namaḥ* |	ॐ मुख्यबिम्बसनातनाय नमः ।
657.	*Oṃ Jīvasañjīvanāya Namaḥ* |	ॐ जीवसञ्जीवनाय नमः
658.	*Oṃ Jīvāya Namaḥ* |	ॐ जीवाय नमः ।
659.	*Oṃ Cidvilāsāya Namaḥ* |	ॐ चिद्विलासाय नमः ।
660.	*Oṃ Cidāśrayāya Namaḥ* |	ॐ चिदाश्रयाय नमः ।
661.	*Oṃ Mahendrāya Namaḥ* |	ॐ महेन्द्राय नमः ।
662.	*Oṃ Amaramānyāya Namaḥ* |	ॐ अमरमान्याय नमः ।
663.	*Oṃ Yogīndrāya Namaḥ* |	ॐ योगीन्द्राय नमः ।
664.	*Oṃ Yogavidmayāya Namaḥ* |	ॐ योगविद्मयाय नमः ।
665.	*Oṃ Yogadharmāya Namaḥ* |	ॐ योगधर्माय नमः ।
666.	*Oṃ Yogāya Namaḥ* |	ॐ योगाय नमः ।
667.	*Oṃ Tattvāya Namaḥ* |	ॐ तत्त्वाय नमः ।

668.	*Oṃ Tattvaviniścayāya Namaḥ* |	ॐ तत्त्वविनिश्चयाय नमः ।
669.	*Oṃ Naikabāhave Namaḥ* |	ॐ नैकबाहवे नमः ।
670.	*Oṃ Anantātmane Namaḥ* |	ॐ अनन्तात्मने नमः ।
671.	*Oṃ Naikanānāparākroṇāya Namaḥ* |	ॐ नैकनानापराक्रोणाय नमः ।
672.	*Oṃ Naikākṣiṇe Namaḥ* |	ॐ नैकाक्षिणे नमः ।
673.	*Oṃ Naikapādāya Namaḥ* |	ॐ नैकपादाय नमः ।
674.	*Oṃ Nāthanāthāya Namaḥ* |	ॐ नाथनाथाय नमः ।
675.	*Oṃ Uttamottamāya Namaḥ* |	ॐ उत्तमोत्तमाय नमः ।
676.	*Oṃ Sahasraśīrṣiṇe Namaḥ* |	ॐ सहस्रशीर्षिणे नमः ।
677.	*Oṃ Puruṣāya Namaḥ* |	ॐ पुरुषाय नमः ।
678.	*Oṃ Sahasrākṣāya Namaḥ* |	ॐ सहस्राक्षाय नमः ।
679.	*Oṃ Sahasrapade Namaḥ* |	ॐ सहस्रपदे नमः ।
680.	*Oṃ Sahasrarūpadṛśe Namaḥ* |	ॐ सहस्ररूपदृशे नमः ।
681.	*Oṃ Sahasrāmaya Udbhavāya Namaḥ* |	ॐ सहस्रामय उद्भवाय नमः ।
682.	*Oṃ Tripāda Puruṣāya Namaḥ* |	ॐ त्रिपाद पुरुषाय नमः ।
683.	*Oṃ Tripadordhvāya Namaḥ* |	ॐ त्रिपदोर्ध्वाय नमः ।
684.	*Oṃ Tryayambakāya Namaḥ* |	ॐ त्र्ययम्बकाय नमः ।
685.	*Oṃ Mahāvīryāya Namaḥ* |	ॐ महावीर्याय नमः ।
686.	*Oṃ Yogavīryaviśāradāya Namaḥ* |	ॐ योगवीर्यविशारदाय नमः ।
687.	*Oṃ Vijayine Namaḥ* |	ॐ विजयिने नमः ।
688.	*Oṃ Vinayine Namaḥ* |	ॐ विनयिने नमः ।
689.	*Oṃ Jetre Namaḥ* |	ॐ जेत्रे नमः ।
690.	*Oṃ Vītarāgiṇe Namaḥ* |	ॐ वीतरागिणे नमः ।
691.	*Oṃ Virājitāya Namaḥ* |	ॐ विराजिताय नमः ।
692.	*Oṃ Rudrāya Namaḥ* |	ॐ रुद्राय नमः ।

693.	*Oṃ Raudrāya Namaḥ* I	ॐ रौद्राय नमः ।
694.	*Oṃ Mahābhīmāya Namaḥ* I	ॐ महाभीमाय नमः ।
695.	*Oṃ Prājñamukhyāya Namaḥ* I	ॐ प्राज्ञमुख्याय नमः ।
696.	*Oṃ Sadāśucaye Namaḥ* I	ॐ सदाशुचये नमः ।
697.	*Oṃ Antarjyotiṣe Namaḥ* I	ॐ अन्तर्ज्योतिषे नमः ।
698.	*Oṃ Anantātmane Namaḥ* I	ॐ अनन्तात्मने नमः ।
699.	*Oṃ Pratyagātmane Namaḥ* I	ॐ प्रत्यगात्मने नमः ।
700.	*Oṃ Nirantarāya Namaḥ* I	ॐ निरन्तराय नमः ।
701.	*Oṃ Arūpāya Namaḥ* I	ॐ अरूपाय नमः ।
702.	*Oṃ Ātmarūpāya Namaḥ* I	ॐ आत्मरूपाय नमः ।
703.	*Oṃ Sarvabhāvavinirvṛttāya Namaḥ* I	ॐ सर्वभावविनिर्वृत्ताय नमः ।
704.	*Oṃ Antaḥśūnyāya Namaḥ* I	ॐ अन्तःशून्याय नमः ।
705.	*Oṃ Bahiḥśūnyāya Namaḥ* I	ॐ बहिःशून्याय नमः ।
706.	*Oṃ Śūnyātmane Namaḥ* I	ॐ शून्यात्मने नमः ।
707.	*Oṃ Śūnyabhāvanāya Namaḥ* I	ॐ शून्यभावनाय नमः ।
708.	*Oṃ Antaḥpūrṇāya Namaḥ* I	ॐ अन्तःपूर्णाय नमः ।
709.	*Oṃ Bahiḥpūrṇāya Namaḥ* I	ॐ बहिःपूर्णाय नमः ।
710.	*Oṃ Pūrṇātmane Namaḥ* I	ॐ पूर्णात्मने नमः ।
711.	*Oṃ Pūrṇabhāvanāya Namaḥ* I	ॐ पूर्णभावनाय नमः ।
712.	*Oṃ Antastyāgine Namaḥ* I	ॐ अन्तस्त्यागिने नमः ।
713.	*Oṃ Bahistyāgine Namaḥ* I	ॐ बहिस्त्यागिने नमः ।
714.	*Oṃ Tyāgātmane Namaḥ* I	ॐ त्यागात्मने नमः ।
715.	*Oṃ Sarvayogavate Namaḥ* I	ॐ सर्वयोगवते नमः ।
716.	*Oṃ Antaryogine Namaḥ* I	ॐ अन्तर्योगिने नमः ।
717.	*Oṃ Bahiryogine Namaḥ* I	ॐ बहिर्योगिने नमः ।
718.	*Oṃ Sarvayogaparāyaṇāya Namaḥ* I	ॐ सर्वयोगपरायणाय नमः ।

719.	*Oṃ Antarbhogine Namaḥ* I	ॐ अन्तर्भोगिने नमः ।
720.	*Oṃ Bahirbhogine Namaḥ* I	ॐ बहिर्भोगिने नमः ।
721.	*Oṃ Sarvabhigaviduttamāya Namaḥ* I	ॐ सर्वभिगविदुत्तमाय नमः ।
722.	*Oṃ Antarniṣṭhāya Namaḥ* I	ॐ अन्तर्निष्ठाय नमः ।
723.	*Oṃ Bahirniṣṭhāya Namaḥ* I	ॐ बहिर्निष्ठाय नमः ।
724.	*Oṃ Sarvaniṣṭhāmayāya Namaḥ* I	ॐ सर्वनिष्ठामयाय नमः ।
725.	*Oṃ Bāhyāntaravimuktāya Namaḥ* I	ॐ बाह्यान्तरविमुक्ताय नमः ।
726.	*Oṃ Bāhyāntaravivarjitāya Namaḥ* I	ॐ बाह्यान्तरविवर्जिताय नमः ।
727.	*Oṃ Śāntāya Namaḥ* I	ॐ शान्ताय नमः ।
728.	*Oṃ Śuddhāya Namaḥ* I	ॐ शुद्धाय नमः ।
729.	*Oṃ Viśuddhāya Namaḥ* I	ॐ विशुद्धाय नमः ।
730.	*Oṃ Nirvāṇāya Namaḥ* I	ॐ निर्वाणाय नमः ।
731.	*Oṃ Prakṛtice Parāya Namaḥ* I	ॐ प्रकृतिचे पराय नमः ।
732.	*Oṃ Akālāya Namaḥ* I	ॐ अकालाय नमः ।
733.	*Oṃ Kālanemine Namaḥ* I	ॐ कालनेमिने नमः ।
734.	*Oṃ Kālakālāya Namaḥ* I	ॐ कालकालाय नमः ।
735.	*Oṃ Janeśvarāya Namaḥ* I	ॐ जनेश्वराय नमः ।
736.	*Oṃ Kālātmane Namaḥ* I	ॐ कालात्मने नमः ।
737.	*Oṃ Kālakartre Namaḥ* I	ॐ कालकर्त्रे नमः ।
738.	*Oṃ Kālajñāya Namaḥ* I	ॐ कालज्ञाय नमः ।
739.	*Oṃ Kālanāśanāya Namaḥ* I	ॐ कालनाशनाय नमः ।
740.	*Oṃ Kaivalypadadātre Namaḥ* I	ॐ कैवल्यपददात्रे नमः ।
741.	*Oṃ Kaivalyasukhadāyakāya Namaḥ* I	ॐ कैवल्यसुखदायकाय नमः ।
742.	*Oṃ Kaivalyālayadharāya Namaḥ* I	ॐ कैवल्यालयधराय नमः ।

743.	*Oṃ Nirbharāya Namaḥ* |	ॐ निर्भराय नमः ।
744.	*Oṃ Harśavardhanāya Namaḥ* |	ॐ हर्शवर्धनाय नमः ।
745.	*Oṃ Hṛdayasthāya Namaḥ* |	ॐ हृदयस्थाय नमः ।
746.	*Oṃ Hṛṣikeṣāya Namaḥ* |	ॐ हृषिकेषाय नमः ।
747.	*Oṃ Govindāya Namaḥ* |	ॐ गोविन्दाय नमः ।
748.	*Oṃ Garbhavarjitāya Namaḥ* |	ॐ गर्भवर्जिताय नमः ।
749.	*Oṃ Sakalāgamapūjyāya Namaḥ* |	ॐ सकलागमपूज्याय नमः ।
750.	*Oṃ Nigamāya Namaḥ* |	ॐ निगमाय नमः ।
751.	*Oṃ Nigamāśrayāya Namaḥ* |	ॐ निगमाश्रयाय नमः ।
752.	*Oṃ Parāśaktaye Namaḥ* |	ॐ पराशक्तये नमः ।
753.	*Oṃ Parākīrtaye Namaḥ* |	ॐ पराकीर्तये नमः ।
754.	*Oṃ Parāvṛttaye Namaḥ* |	ॐ परावृत्तये नमः ।
755.	*Oṃ Nidhismṛtaye Namaḥ* |	ॐ निधिस्मृतये नमः ।
756.	*Oṃ Parāvidyā Parākṣāntaye Namaḥ* |	ॐ पराविद्या पराक्षान्तये नमः ।
757.	*Oṃ Vibhaktaye Namaḥ* |	ॐ विभक्तये नमः ।
758.	*Oṃ Yuktasadgataye Namaḥ* |	ॐ युक्तसद्गतये नमः ।
759.	*Oṃ Svaprakāśāya Namaḥ* |	ॐ स्वप्रकाशाय नमः ।
760.	*Oṃ Prakāśātmane Namaḥ* |	ॐ प्रकाशात्मने नमः ।
761.	*Oṃ Parāsaṃvedanātmakāya Namaḥ* |	ॐ परासंवेदनात्मकाय नमः ।
762.	*Oṃ Svasevyāya Namaḥ* |	ॐ स्वसेव्याय नमः ।
763.	*Oṃ Svavidaṃ Svātmane Namaḥ* |	ॐ स्वविदं स्वात्मने नमः।
764.	*Oṃ Svasaṃvedyāya Namaḥ* |	ॐ स्वसंवेद्याय नमः ।
765.	*Oṃ Anaghāya Namaḥ* |	ॐ अनघाय नमः ।
766.	*Oṃ Kṣamiṇe Namaḥ* |	ॐ क्षमिणे नमः ।

767.	*Oṃ Svānusandhāna Śīlātmane Namaḥ* I	ॐ स्वानुसन्धान शीलात्मने नमः ।
768.	*Oṃ Svānusandhāna Gocarāya Namaḥ* I	ॐ स्वानुसन्धान गोचराय नमः ।
769.	*Oṃ Svānusandhāna Śūnyātmane Namaḥ* I	ॐ स्वानुसन्धान शून्यात्मने नमः ।
770.	*Oṃ Svanusandhānāśrayāya Namaḥ* I	ॐ स्वनुसन्धानाश्रयाय नमः ।
771.	*Oṃ Svabodhadarpaṇāya Namaḥ* I	ॐ स्वबोधदर्पणाय नमः ।
772.	*Oṃ Abhaṅgāya Namaḥ* I	ॐ अभङ्गाय नमः ।
773.	*Oṃ Kandarpakulanāśanāya Namaḥ* I	ॐ कन्दर्पकुलनाशनाय नमः ।
774.	*Oṃ Brahmacāriṇe Namaḥ* I	ॐ ब्रह्मचारिणे नमः ।
775.	*Oṃ Brahmavetre Namaḥ* I	ॐ ब्रह्मवेत्रे नमः ।
776.	*Oṃ Brāhmaṇāya Namaḥ* I	ॐ ब्राह्मणाय नमः ।
777.	*Oṃ Brahmavittamāya Namaḥ* I	ॐ ब्रह्मवित्तमाय नमः ।
778.	*Oṃ Tattvabodhāya Namaḥ* I	ॐ तत्त्वबोधाय नमः ।
779.	*Oṃ Sudhāvarṣāya Namaḥ* I	ॐ सुधावर्षाय नमः ।
780.	*Oṃ Pavanāya Namaḥ* I	ॐ पवनाय नमः ।
781.	*Oṃ Pāpapāvakāya Namaḥ* I	ॐ पापपावकाय नमः ।
782.	*Oṃ Brahmasūtravidheyātmane Namaḥ* I	ॐ ब्रह्मसूत्रविधेयात्मने नमः ।
783.	*Oṃ Brahmasūtrārthanirṇayāya Namaḥ* I	ॐ ब्रह्मसूत्रार्थनिर्णयाय नमः ।
784.	*Oṃ Atyantikāya Namaḥ* I	ॐ अत्यन्तिकाय नमः ।
785.	*Oṃ Mahākalpāya Namaḥ* I	ॐ महाकल्पाय नमः ।
786.	*Oṃ Saṅkalpāvarta Nāśanāya Namaḥ* I	ॐ सङ्कल्पावर्त नाशनाय नमः ।

787.	*Oṃ Ādhivyādhiharāya Namaḥ* I	ॐ आधिव्याधिहराय नमः ।
788.	*Oṃ Saṃśayārṇava Śoṣakāya Namaḥ* I	ॐ संशयार्णव शोषकाय नमः ।
789.	*Oṃ Tattvātmajñānasandeśāya Namaḥ* I	ॐ तत्त्वात्मज्ञानसन्देशाय नमः ।
790.	*Oṃ Mahānubhāvabhāvitāya Namaḥ* I	ॐ महानुभावभाविताय नमः ।
791.	*Oṃ Ātmānubhavasampannāya Namaḥ* I	ॐ आत्मानुभवसम्पन्नाय नमः ।
792.	*Oṃ Svānubhavasukhāśrayāya Namaḥ* I	ॐ स्वानुभवसुखाश्रयाय नमः ।
793.	*Oṃ Acintyāya Namaḥ* I	ॐ अचिन्त्याय नमः ।
794.	*Oṃ Bṛhadbhānave Namaḥ* I	ॐ बृहद्भानवे नमः ।
795.	*Oṃ Pramadotkarṣanāśanāya Namaḥ* I	ॐ प्रमदोत्कर्षनाशनाय नमः ।
796.	*Oṃ Aniketa Praśāntātmane Namaḥ* I	ॐ अनिकेत प्रशान्तात्मने नमः ।
797.	*Oṃ Śūnyavāsāya Namaḥ* I	ॐ शून्यवासाय नमः ।
798.	*Oṃ Jagadvapuṣe Namaḥ* I	ॐ जगद्वपुषे नमः ।
799.	*Oṃ Cidgataye Namaḥ* I	ॐ चिद्गतये नमः ।
800.	*Oṃ Cinmayāya Namaḥ* I	ॐ चिन्मयाय नमः ।
801.	*Oṃ Cakriṇe* I	ॐ चक्रिणे ।
802.	*Oṃ Māyācakrapravartakāya Namaḥ* I	ॐ मायाचक्रप्रवर्तकाय नमः ।
803.	*Oṃ Sarvavarṇavidārambhiṇe Namaḥ* I	ॐ सर्ववर्णविदारम्भिणे नमः ।
804.	*Oṃ Sarvārambhaparāyaṇāya Namaḥ* I	ॐ सर्वारम्भपरायणाय नमः ।
805.	*Oṃ Purāṇāya Namaḥ* I	ॐ पुराणाय नमः ।

806.	*Oṃ Pravarāya Namaḥ* |	ॐ प्रवराय नमः ।
807.	*Oṃ Dātre Namaḥ* |	ॐ दात्रे नमः ।
808.	*Oṃ Sunarāya Namaḥ* |	ॐ सुनराय नमः ।
809.	*Oṃ Kanakāṅgadine Namaḥ* |	ॐ कनकाङ्गदिने नमः ।
810.	*Oṃ Anasūyātmajāya Namaḥ* |	ॐ अनसूयात्मजाय नमः।
811.	*Oṃ Dattāya Namaḥ* |	ॐ दत्ताय नमः ।
812.	*Oṃ Sarvajñāya Namaḥ* |	ॐ सर्वज्ञाय नमः ।
813.	*Oṃ Sarvakāmadāya Namaḥ* |	ॐ सर्वकामदाय नमः ।
814.	*Oṃ Kāmajite Namaḥ* |	ॐ कामजिते नमः ।
815.	*Oṃ Kāmapaṭāya Namaḥ* |	ॐ कामपटाय नमः ।
816.	*Oṃ Kāmine Namaḥ* |	ॐ कामिने नमः ।
817.	*Oṃ Kāmapradāgamāya Namaḥ* |	ॐ कामप्रदागमाय नमः ।
818.	*Oṃ Kāmavate Namaḥ* |	ॐ कामवते नमः ।
819.	*Oṃ Kāmapoṣāya Namaḥ* |	ॐ कामपोषाय नमः ।
820.	*Oṃ Sarvakāmanivartakāya Namaḥ* |	ॐ सर्वकामनिवर्तकाय नमः ।
821.	*Oṃ Sarvakāmaphalotpattaye Namaḥ* |	ॐ सर्वकामफलोत्पत्तये नमः ।
822.	*Oṃ Sarvakāmaphalapradāya Namaḥ* |	ॐ सर्वकामफलप्रदाय नमः ।
823.	*Oṃ Sarvakāmaphalaiḥ Pūjyāya Namaḥ* |	ॐ सर्वकामफलैः पूज्याय नमः ।
824.	*Oṃ Sarvakāmaphalāśrayāya Namaḥ* |	ॐ सर्वकामफलाश्रयाय नमः ।
825.	*Oṃ Viśvakarmaṇe Namaḥ* |	ॐ विश्वकर्मणे नमः ।
826.	*Oṃ Kṛtātmane Namaḥ* |	ॐ कृतात्मने नमः ।
827.	*Oṃ Kṛtajñāya Namaḥ* |	ॐ कृतज्ञाय नमः ।
828.	*Oṃ Sarvasākṣikāya Namaḥ* |	ॐ सर्वसाक्षिकाय नमः ।

829.	*Oṃ Sarvārambhaparityāgine Namaḥ* |	ॐ सर्वारम्भपरित्यागिने नमः ।
830.	*Oṃ Jaḍonmattapiśācavate Namaḥ* |	ॐ जडोन्मत्तपिशाचवते नमः ।
831.	*Oṃ Bhikṣave Namaḥ* |	ॐ भिक्षवे नमः ।
832.	*Oṃ Bhikṣākarāya Namaḥ* |	ॐ भिक्षाकराय नमः ।
833.	*Oṃ Bhīkṣṇāhāriṇe Namaḥ* |	ॐ भीक्ष्णाहारिणे नमः ।
834.	*Oṃ Nirāśramaṇe Namaḥ* |	ॐ निराश्रमणे नमः ।
835.	*Oṃ Akulāya Namaḥ* |	ॐ अकुलाय नमः ।
836.	*Oṃ Anukūlāya Namaḥ* |	ॐ अनुकूलाय नमः ।
837.	*Oṃ Vikalāya Namaḥ* |	ॐ विकलाय नमः ।
838.	*Oṃ Akalāya Namaḥ* |	ॐ अकलाय नमः ।
839.	*Oṃ Jaṭilāya Namaḥ* |	ॐ जटिलाय नमः ।
840.	*Oṃ Vanacāriṇe Namaḥ* |	ॐ वनचारिणे नमः ।
841.	*Oṃ Daṇḍine Namaḥ* |	ॐ दण्डिने नमः ।
842.	*Oṃ Muṇḍine Namaḥ* |	ॐ मुण्डिने नमः ।
843.	*Oṃ Gandhine Namaḥ* |	ॐ गन्धिने नमः ।
844.	*Oṃ Dehadharmavihīnātmane Namaḥ* |	ॐ देहधर्मविहीनात्मने नमः ।
845.	*Oṃ Ekākine Namaḥ* |	ॐ एकाकिने नमः ।
846.	*Oṃ Saṅgavarjitāya Namaḥ* |	ॐ सङ्गवर्जिताय नमः ।
847.	*Oṃ Āśramiṇe Namaḥ* |	ॐ आश्रमिणे नमः ।
848.	*Oṃ Anāśramārambhāya Namaḥ* |	ॐ अनाश्रमारम्भाय नमः।
849.	*Oṃ Anācāriṇe Namaḥ* |	ॐ अनाचारिणे नमः ।
850.	*Oṃ Karmavarjitāya Namaḥ* |	ॐ कर्मवर्जिताय नमः ।
851.	*Oṃ Asandehine Namaḥ* |	ॐ असन्देहिने नमः ।
852.	*Oṃ Sandehine Namaḥ* |	ॐ सन्देहिने नमः ।

853.	*Oṃ Nakiñcanāya Namaḥ* |	ॐ नकिञ्चनाय नमः ।
854.	*Oṃ Nṛdehine Namaḥ* |	ॐ नृदेहिने नमः ।
855.	*Oṃ Dehaśūnyāya Namaḥ* |	ॐ देहशून्याय नमः ।
856.	*Oṃ Nābhāvine Namaḥ* |	ॐ नाभाविने नमः ।
857.	*Oṃ Bhāvanirgatāya Namaḥ* |	ॐ भावनिर्गताय नमः ।
858.	*Oṃ Nābrahmaṇe Namaḥ* |	ॐ नाब्रह्मणे नमः ।
859.	*Oṃ Parabrahmaṇe Namaḥ* |	ॐ परब्रह्मणे नमः ।
860.	*Oṃ Svayameva Nirākulāya Namaḥ* |	ॐ स्वयमेव निराकुलाय नमः ।
861.	*Oṃ Anaghāya Namaḥ* |	ॐ अनघाय नमः ।
862.	*Oṃ Agurave Namaḥ* |	ॐ अगुरवे नमः ।
863.	*Oṃ Nāthanāthottamāya Namaḥ* |	ॐ नाथनाथोत्तमाय नमः ।
864.	*Oṃ Gurave Namaḥ* |	ॐ गुरवे नमः ।
865.	*Oṃ Dvibhujāya Namaḥ* |	ॐ द्विभुजाय नमः ।
866.	*Oṃ Prākṛtāya Namaḥ* |	ॐ प्राकृताय नमः ।
867.	*Oṃ Janakāya Namaḥ* |	ॐ जनकाय नमः ।
868.	*Oṃ Pitāmahāya Namaḥ* |	ॐ पितामहाय नमः ।
869.	*Oṃ Anātmane Namaḥ* |	ॐ अनात्मने नमः ।
870.	*Oṃ Nacanānātmane Namaḥ* |	ॐ नचनानात्मने नमः ।
871.	*Oṃ Nītaye Namaḥ* |	ॐ नीतये नमः ।
872.	*Oṃ Nītimatāṃ Varāya Namaḥ* |	ॐ नीतिमतां वराय नमः ।
873.	*Oṃ Sahajāya Namaḥ* |	ॐ सहजाय नमः ।
874.	*Oṃ Sadṛśāya Namaḥ* |	ॐ सदृशाय नमः ।
875.	*Oṃ Siddhāya Namaḥ* |	ॐ सिद्धाय नमः ।
876.	*Oṃ Ekāya Namaḥ* |	ॐ एकाय नमः ।
877.	*Oṃ Cinmātrāya Namaḥ* |	ॐ चिन्मात्राय नमः ।
878.	*Oṃ Nakartre Namaḥ* |	ॐ नकर्त्रे नमः ।
879.	*Oṃ Kartre Namaḥ* |	ॐ कर्त्रे नमः ।

880.	Oṃ Bhoktre Namaḥ |	ॐ भोक्त्रे नमः ।
881.	Oṃ Bhogavivarjitāya Namaḥ |	ॐ भोगविवर्जिताय नमः ।
882.	Oṃ Turīyāya Namaḥ |	ॐ तुरीयाय नमः ।
883.	Oṃ Turīyātītāya Namaḥ |	ॐ तुरीयातीताय नमः ।
884.	Oṃ Svacchāya Namaḥ |	ॐ स्वच्छाय नमः ।
885.	Oṃ Sarvamayāya Namaḥ |	ॐ सर्वमयाय नमः ।
886.	Oṃ Sarvādhiṣṭhānarūpaya Namaḥ |	ॐ सर्वाधिष्ठानरूपय नमः ।
887.	Oṃ Sarvadhyeyavivarjitāya Namaḥ |	ॐ सर्वध्येयविवर्जिताय नमः ।
888.	Oṃ Sarvalokanivāsātmane Namaḥ |	ॐ सर्वलोकनिवासात्मने नमः ।
889.	Oṃ Sakalottamavanditāya Namaḥ	ॐ सकलोत्तमवन्दिताय नमः
890.	Oṃ Dehabhṛte Namaḥ |	ॐ देहभृते नमः ।
891.	Oṃ Dehakṛte Namaḥ |	ॐ देहकृते नमः ।
892.	Oṃ Dehātmane Namaḥ |	ॐ देहात्मने नमः ।
893.	Oṃ Dehabhāvanāya Namaḥ |	ॐ देहभावनाय नमः ।
894.	Oṃ Dehine Namaḥ |	ॐ देहिने नमः ।
895.	Oṃ Dehavibhaktāya Namaḥ |	ॐ देहविभक्ताय नमः ।
896.	Oṃ Dehabhāvaprakāśanāya Namaḥ |	ॐ देहभावप्रकाशनाय नमः ।
897.	Oṃ Layasthāya Namaḥ |	ॐ लयस्थाय नमः ।
898.	Oṃ Layavide Namaḥ |	ॐ लयविदे नमः ।
899.	Oṃ Layabhāvāya Namaḥ |	ॐ लयभावाय नमः ।
900.	Oṃ Bodhavate Namaḥ |	ॐ बोधवते नमः ।
901.	Oṃ Layātītāya Namaḥ |	ॐ लयातीताय नमः ।
902.	Oṃ Layasyāntāya Namaḥ |	ॐ लयस्यान्ताय नमः ।
903.	Oṃ Layabhāvanivāraṇāya Namaḥ	ॐ लयभावनिवारणाय नमः ।
904.	Oṃ Vimukhāya Namaḥ |	ॐ विमुखाय नमः ।

905.	*Oṃ Pramukhāya Namaḥ* I	ॐ प्रमुखाय नमः ।
906.	*Oṃ Pratyaṅmukhavadācāriṇe Namaḥ* I	ॐ प्रत्यङ्मुखवदाचारिणे नमः ।
907.	*Oṃ Viśvabhuje Namaḥ* I	ॐ विश्वभुजे नमः ।
908.	*Oṃ Viśvaghṛṣe Namaḥ* I	ॐ विश्वघृषे नमः ।
909.	*Oṃ Viśvāya Namaḥ* I	ॐ विश्वाय नमः ।
910.	*Oṃ Viśvakṣemakarāya Namaḥ* I	ॐ विश्वक्षेमकराय नमः ।
911.	*Oṃ Avikṣiptāya Namaḥ* I	ॐ अविक्षिप्ताय नमः ।
912.	*Oṃ Apramādine Namaḥ* I	ॐ अप्रमादिने नमः ।
913.	*Oṃ Parārdhaye Namaḥ* I	ॐ परार्धये नमः ।
914.	*Oṃ Paramārthadṛśe Namaḥ* I	ॐ परमार्थदृशे नमः ।
915.	*Oṃ Svānubhavavihīnāya Namaḥ* I	ॐ स्वानुभवविहीनाय नमः ।
916.	*Oṃ Svānubhavaprakāśanāya Namaḥ* I	ॐ स्वानुभवप्रकाशनाय नमः ।
917.	*Oṃ Nirindriyāya Namaḥ* I	ॐ निरिन्द्रियाय नमः ।
918.	*Oṃ Nirbuddhaye Namaḥ* I	ॐ निर्बुद्धये नमः ।
919.	*Oṃ Nirābhāsāya Namaḥ* I	ॐ निराभासाय नमः ।
920.	*Oṃ Nirākṛtāya Namaḥ* I	ॐ निराकृताय नमः ।
921.	*Oṃ Nirahaṅkārāya Namaḥ* I	ॐ निरहङ्काराय नमः ।
922.	*Oṃ Rūpātmane Namaḥ* I	ॐ रूपात्मने नमः ।
923.	*Oṃ Nirvapuṣe Namaḥ* I	ॐ निर्वपुषे नमः ।
924.	*Oṃ Sakalāśrayāya Namaḥ* I	ॐ सकलाश्रयाय नमः ।
925.	*Oṃ Śokaduḥkhaharāya Namaḥ* I	ॐ शोकदुःखहराय नमः ।
926.	*Oṃ Bhogamokṣaphalapradāya Namaḥ* I	ॐ भोगमोक्षफलप्रदाय नमः ।
927.	*Oṃ Suprasannāya Namaḥ* I	ॐ सुप्रसन्नाय नमः ।
928.	*Oṃ Sūkṣmāya Namaḥ* I	ॐ सूक्ष्माय नमः ।

929.	*Oṃ Śabdabrahmārthasaṃgṛhāya Namaḥ* |	ॐ शब्दब्रह्मार्थसंगृहाय नमः ।
930.	*Oṃ Āgamāpāya Śūnyāya Namaḥ* |	ॐ आगमापाय शून्याय नमः।
931.	*Oṃ Sthānadāya Namaḥ* |	ॐ स्थानदाय नमः ।
932.	*Oṃ Satāṅgataye Namaḥ* |	ॐ सताङ्गतये नमः ।
933.	*Oṃ Ākṛtāya Namaḥ* |	ॐ आकृताय नमः ।
934.	*Oṃ Sukṛtāya Namaḥ* |	ॐ सुकृताय नमः ।
935.	*Oṃ Kṛtakarmavinirvṛtāya Namaḥ* |	ॐ कृतकर्मविनिर्वृताय नमः ।
936.	*Oṃ Bhedatrayaharāya Namaḥ* |	ॐ भेदत्रयहराय नमः ।
937.	*Oṃ Dehatrayavinirgatāya Namaḥ* |	ॐ देहत्रयविनिर्गताय नमः ।
938.	*Oṃ Sarvakāmapradāya Namaḥ* |	ॐ सर्वकामप्रदाय नमः ।
939.	*Oṃ Sarvakāmanivartakāya Namaḥ* |	ॐ सर्वकामनिवर्तकाय नमः ।
940.	*Oṃ Siddheśvarāya Namaḥ* |	ॐ सिद्धेश्वराय नमः ।
941.	*Oṃ Ajarāya Namaḥ* |	ॐ अजराय नमः ।
942.	*Oṃ Pañcabāṇadarpahutāśanāya Namaḥ* |	ॐ पञ्चबाणदर्पहुताशनाय नमः ।
943.	*Oṃ Caturākṣarabījātmane Namaḥ*	ॐ चतुराक्षरबीजात्मने नमः ।
944.	*Oṃ Svabhuve Namaḥ* |	ॐ स्वभुवे नमः ।
945.	*Oṃ Citkīrtibhūṣaṇāya Namaḥ* |	ॐ चित्कीर्तिभूषणाय नमः ।
946.	*Oṃ Agādhabuddhaye Namaḥ* |	ॐ अगाधबुद्धये नमः ।
947.	*Oṃ Akṣubdhāya Namaḥ* |	ॐ अक्षुब्धाय नमः ।
948.	*Oṃ Candrasūryāgnilocanāya Namaḥ* |	ॐ चन्द्रसूर्याग्निलोचनाय नमः ।
949.	*Oṃ Yamadaṃṣṭrāya Namaḥ* |	ॐ यमदंष्ट्राय नमः ।
950.	*Oṃ Atisaṃhartre Namaḥ* |	ॐ अतिसंहर्त्रे नमः ।
951.	*Oṃ Paramānandasāgarāya Namaḥ* |	ॐ परमानन्दसागराय नमः ।
952.	*Oṃ Līlāviśvambharāya Namaḥ* |	ॐ लीलाविश्वम्भराय नमः ।

953.	*Oṃ Bhānave Namaḥ* |	ॐ भानवे नमः ।
954.	*Oṃ Bhairavāya Namaḥ* |	ॐ भैरवाय नमः ।
955.	*Oṃ Bhīmalocanāya Namaḥ* |	ॐ भीमलोचनाय नमः ।
956.	*Oṃ Brahmacarmāmbarāya Namaḥ* |	ॐ ब्रह्मचर्माम्बराय नमः ।
957.	*Oṃ Kālāya Namaḥ* |	ॐ कालाय नमः ।
958.	*Oṃ Acalāya Namaḥ* |	ॐ अचलाय नमः ।
959.	*Oṃ Calanāntakāya Namaḥ* |	ॐ चलनान्तकाय नमः ।
960.	*Oṃ Ādidevāya Namaḥ* |	ॐ आदिदेवाय नमः ।
961.	*Oṃ Jagadyonaye Namaḥ* |	ॐ जगद्योनये नमः ।
962.	*Oṃ Vāsavāri Vimardanāya Namaḥ*	ॐ वासवारि विमर्दनाय नमः।
963.	*Oṃ Vikarmakarmakarmajñāya Namaḥ* |	ॐ विकर्मकर्मकर्मज्ञाय नमः ।
964.	*Oṃ Ananya Gamakāya Namaḥ* |	ॐ अनन्य गमकाय नमः ।
965.	*Oṃ Agamāya Namaḥ* |	ॐ अगमाय नमः ।
966.	*Oṃ Abaddhakarmaśūnyāya Namaḥ* |	ॐ अबद्धकर्मशून्याय नमः ।
967.	*Oṃ Kāmarāgakulakṣayāya Namaḥ*	ॐ कामरागकुलक्षयाय नमः।
968.	*Oṃ Yogāndhakāramathanāya Namaḥ* |	ॐ योगान्धकारमथनाय नमः ।
969.	*Oṃ Padmajanmādivanditāya Namaḥ* |	ॐ पद्मजन्मादिवन्दिताय नमः ।
970.	*Oṃ Bhaktakāmāya Namaḥ* |	ॐ भक्तकामाय नमः ।
971.	*Oṃ Agrajāya Namaḥ* |	ॐ अग्रजाय नमः ।
972.	*Oṃ Cakriṇe Namaḥ* |	ॐ चक्रिणे नमः ।
973.	*Oṃ Bhāvanirbhāvakāya Namaḥ* |	ॐ भावनिर्भावकाय नमः ।
974.	*Oṃ Bhedāṅkāya Namaḥ* |	ॐ भेदाङ्काय नमः ।
975.	*Oṃ Mahate Namaḥ* |	ॐ महते नमः ।
976.	*Oṃ Agragāya Namaḥ* |	ॐ अग्रगाय नमः ।

977.	*Oṃ Niguhāya Namaḥ* I	ॐ निगुहाय नमः ।
978.	*Oṃ Gocarāntakāya Namaḥ* I	ॐ गोचरान्तकाय नमः ।
979.	*Oṃ Kālāgniśamanāya Namaḥ* I	ॐ कालाग्निशमनाय नमः ।
980.	*Oṃ Śaṅkha Cakra Ppadma Gadādharāya Namaḥ* I	ॐ शङ्खचक्रपद्मगदाधराय नमः ।
981.	*Oṃ Dīptāya Namaḥ* I	ॐ दीप्ताय नमः ।
982.	*Oṃ Dīnapataye Namaḥ* I	ॐ दीनपतये नमः ।
983.	*Oṃ Śāstre Namaḥ* I	ॐ शास्त्रे नमः ।
984.	*Oṃ Svacchandāya Namaḥ* I	ॐ स्वच्छन्दाय नमः ।
985.	*Oṃ Muktidāyakāya Namaḥ* I	ॐ मुक्तिदायकाय नमः ।
986.	*Oṃ Vyomadharmāmbarāya Namaḥ* I	ॐ व्योमधर्माम्बराय नमः ।
987.	*Oṃ Bhettre Namaḥ* I	ॐ भेत्त्रे नमः ।
988.	*Oṃ Bhasmadhāriṇe Namaḥ* I	ॐ भस्मधारिणे नमः ।
989.	*Oṃ Dharādharāya Namaḥ* I	ॐ धराधराय नमः ।
990.	*Oṃ Dharmaguptāya Namaḥ* I	ॐ धर्मगुप्ताय नमः ।
991.	*Oṃ Anvayātmane Namaḥ* I	ॐ अन्वयात्मने नमः ।
992.	*Oṃ Vyatirekārthanirṇayāya Namaḥ* I	ॐ व्यतिरेकार्थनिर्णयाय नमः ।
993.	*Oṃ Ekoneka Guṇabhāsā Bhāsa Nirbhāsavarjitāya Namaḥ* I	ॐ एकोनेक गुणभासा भास निर्भासवर्जिताय नमः ।
994.	*Oṃ Bhāvābhāva Svabhāvātmane Namaḥ* I	ॐ भावाभाव स्वभावात्मने नमः ।
995.	*Oṃ Bhāvābhāva Vibhāvavide Namaḥ* I	ॐ भावाभाव विभावविदे नमः ।
996.	*Oṃ Yogīhṛdayaviśrāmāya Namaḥ* I	ॐ योगीहृदयविश्रामाय नमः।
997.	*Oṃ Anantavidyāvivardhanāya Namaḥ* I	ॐ अनन्तविद्याविवर्धनाय नमः ।
998.	*Oṃ Vighnāntakāya Namaḥ* I	ॐ विघ्नान्तकाय नमः ।

999.	*Oṃ Trikālajñāya Namaḥ* I	ॐ त्रिकालज्ञाय नमः ।
1000.	*Oṃ Tattvātmajñānasāgarāya Namaḥ* I	ॐ तत्त्वात्मज्ञानसागराय नमः ।

Iti Śrīmad Dattātreya Sahasranāmāvalī Sampūrṇam ||

इति श्रीमद् दत्तात्रेय सहस्रनामावली सम्पूर्णम् ॥

About the Author

(http://Ramamurthy.jaagruti.co.in)

Dr. Ramamurthy is a versatile personality having experience and expertise in various areas of banking, related IT solutions, information security, IT audit, Vedas, Samskrutam and so on.

His thirst for continuous learning does not subside. Even at the age of late fifties, he did research on a unique topic "Information Technology and Samskrutam" and obtained Ph.D. – doctorate degree from University of Madras. He is into a project of developing a Samskrutam based compiler.

It is his passion to spread his knowledge and experience through conducting classes, training programs and writing books.

He has already published books as detailed below. Further books are in pipe-line.

#	Title	Remarks	Pages
		Indology Related	
1.	*Shrī Lalitā Sahasranāmam*	English Translation of Shrī *Bhāskararāya's Bhāśyam*	750
2.	Power of *Shrī Vidyā*	The Secrets Demystified – With Lucid English Rendering and Commentaries	80
3.	ஸ்ரீ வித்யையின் ஶக்தி	ஸ்ரீ வித்யா ரகசியங்கள்	100
4.	*Samatā* – समता	An Exposition of Similarities in *Lalitā Sahasranāma* with *Soundaryalaharī, Saptaśatī, Viśṇu Sahasranāma* and *Shrīmad Bhagavad Gīta*	172
5.	ஸமதா – समता	ஸ்ரீ லலிதா ஸஹஸ்ரநாமம் ஸௌந்தர்யலஹரீ, ஸப்தஶதீ, ஸ்ரீ விஷ்ணு ஸஹஸ்ரநாமம் மற்றும் ஸ்ரீமத் பகவத் கீதைகளில் ஒற்றுமையின் ஒரு வெளிப்பாடு	266
6.	*Advaita* In *Shākta*	Advaita Philosophy Discussed in Shakta Related Books	80
7.	*Shrī Lalitā Triśatī*	300 Divine Names of The Celestial Mother – **English** Translation of *Shrī Ādhi Śaṅkara's Bhāśyam*	193
8.	ஸ்ரீ லலிதா த்ரிஶதி	300 Divine Names of The Celestial Mother – Tamil Translation of *Shrī Ādi Śaṅkara's Bhāśyam*	234

#	Title	Remarks	Pages
9.	Secrets of *Mahāśakti*	Chandi Demystified	78
10.	*Daśa Mahā Vidyā*	Ten Cosmic Forms of The Divine Mother	60
11.	ஸ்ரீ வித்யா பேதங்கள்	ஸ்ரீவித்யா உபாசனையின் படிகள் - கோவை ஶதச் சண்டி மலர்	51
12.	*Shrīvidya* Variances	Variances In Srividya Upasana	50
13.	ஸ்ரீ தேவீ ஸ்துதிகள்	பல முக்கிய அம்பாள் ஸ்தோத்ரங்கள்	133
14.	Śrī Devī Stutis – श्रीदेवी स्तुति:	Various Important Stotras of Sri Devi	223
15.	ஷண்மத மந்த்ரங்கள்	பொள்ளாச்சி ஸ்ரீ ஸஹஸ்ரசண்டீ மஹாயாக நினைவு மலர்	145
16.	*Śanmata Mantras* – षण्मत मन्त्रा:	Important Mantras Relating to Gods of Six Religions	87
17.	தேவதா மந்த்ரங்கள்	அக்கரைப்பட்டி ஸஹஸ்ரசண்டீ மஹாயாக நினைவு மலர்	32
18.	ஆதி ஶங்கரரும் ஷண்மதமும்	ஷண்மதங்களைப் பற்றிய ஒரு அறிமுகம்	32
19.	ஸ்ரீ ஷண்மத தேவதா அர்ச்சனை	ஸ்ரீ மஹா கும்பாபிஷேக மலர்	64
20.	*Vaidhīka* Wedding	Typical Wedding Process in English	56
21.	வைதீகத் திருமணம்	Typical Wedding Process in Tamil	57
22.	ஸ்ரீகுரு பாத பூஜா விதானம்	சித்தகிரி ஸஹஸ்ரசண்டீ மலர்	44
23.	குரு வார வழிபாடு		70
24.	ஸ்ரீவித்யா ஶடாம்னாய மந்த்ரங்கள்	சித்தகிரி ஸஹஸ்ரசண்டீ மலர்	60
25.	*Ekatā*	Oneness Among Shiva, *Viṣṇu* and Shakti	277
26.	ஏகதா - एकता	ஶிவபெருமான், விஷ்ணு மற்றும் ஶக்திக்குள் ஒற்றுமை	370
27.	*Vedas* – An Analytical Perspective	A Description of Veda, Vedanta, Vedanga, Jyotisha, Shastra, Etc.	240
28.	வேதங்கள் - ஒரு பகுப்பாய்வு	A Description of Veda, Vedanta, Vedanga, Jyotisha, Shastra, Etc.	280
29.	பரமாச்சார்யாள் நோக்கில் ஸ்ரீ லலிதாம்பிகா	The Explanation Given by Paramacharya on Some of The Names in Lalitā Sahasranama	175
30.	*Ṣaṇṇavati Tarpaṇa*	Repaying Debts to Ancestors	42
31.	ஷண்ணவதி தர்பணம்	முன்னோர் கடன் தீர்த்தல்	48
32.	*Shrī Mahā Pratyangirā Devī*	Holy Divine Mother in Ferocious Form	41
33.	ஸ்ரீ மஹா ப்ரத்யங்கிரா தேவீ	தெய்வீக அன்னையின் பயங்கர வடிவம்	51
34.	*Śrī Chakra Navāvarṇam*	Marvels of *Śrī Chakra*	115
35.	ஸ்ரீ சக்ர நவாவர்ணம்	ஸ்ரீ சக்ரத்தின் அதிசயங்கள்	130

#	Title	Remarks	Pages
36.	அம்பிகையின் (திரு) அவதாரங்கள்	ஸ்ரீ தேவியின் பல்வேறு அவதாரங்கள்	142
37.	Incarnations of Holy Mother	Different Incarnations of *Śrī Devī*	140
38.	ஸ்ரீ பிரணவானந்தர் - ஒரு சரிதம்	ஒரு அரிய ஸ்வாமிகளின் திவ்ய சரிதம்	121
39.	ஸன்யாஸம் - ஓர் அலசல்	ஹிந்து மத ஸன்யாஸ பேதங்கள் - ஒரு பகுப்பாய்வு	140
40.	Asceticism – An Analysis	A Study of Hindu *Sanyasam*	140
41.	ஶாந்தமும் ப்ரணவமும்	(ஸ்ரீ ஶாந்தானந்தரும் ஸ்ரீ ப்ரணவானந்தரும்) குரு சிஷ்யருக்கு உபதேசங்கள்	120
42.	ஸ்ரீ ஸஹஸ்ராக்ஷரீ வித்யா	2020 சாதுர்மாஸ்ய மலர்	84
43.	*Shakta Upanishats*	*Upanishats* About *Sri Devi*	385
44.	ஶாக்த உபநிஷதங்கள்	*Upanishats* About *Sri Devi*	400
45.	ஸ்ரீ தேவீ கீதை	Sri Devi Geeta	194
46.	*Śrī Devī Gīta*	Sri Devi Geeta	180
47.	*Śrī Gāyatrī Sahasranamam*	1,000 Divine Names of *Śrī Gāyatrī Mātā*	392
48.	ஸ்ரீ காயத்ரீ ஸஹஸ்ரநாமம்	ஸ்ரீ காயத்ரி மாதாவின் 1,000 திவ்ய நாமங்கள்	450
49.	ஸ்ரீ ஸௌந்தர்யலஹரீ - ஒரு உள் அறிவு	ஒரு உள்-அறிவு	250
50.	*Śrī Soundaryalaharī* – an Insight	An Insight	200
51.	ஸ்ரீ ஶிவானந்த^{3}லஹரீ- ஒரு உள் அறிவு	ஒரு உள்-அறிவு	176
52.	*Śrī Śivānandalaharī* – an Insight	An Insight	129
53.	*Śrī Vārāhī Devī*	Holy Divine Mother with A Hog Face	96
54.	ஸ்ரீ வாராஹீ தேவீ	பன்றி முகத்துடன் கூடிய புனிதத் தெய்வீக அன்னை	106
55.	Śrī Vijaya Bhairavar	A Terrifying, Sacred, Divine Form of Lord Shiva	164
56.	ஸ்ரீ விஜய பை$_{4}$ரவர்	ஶிவபெருமானின் ஒரு திகிலூட்டும் புனித தெய்வீக உருவம்	188
57.	ஸ்ரீ ப$_{4}$த்$_{3}$ர காளீ	ஸ்ரீ தேவியின் ஒரு திகிலூட்டும் புனித தெய்வீக உருவம் – 1st Devi of Dasha Maha Vidya	226
58.	*Śrī Bhadra Kālī*	A Startling, Sacred and Divine Form of *Śrī Devī* – 1st Devi of Dasha Maha Vidya	224
59.	திதி^{2} நித்யா தே^{3}விகள்	16 *Tithi Nitya Devis*	230
60.	*Tithi Nityā Devis*	16 *Tithi Nitya Devis*	186
61.	ஸ்ரீ தாரா – நீல ஸரஸ்வதீ	2nd Devi of Dasha Maha Vidya	182
62.	*Śrī Tārā Devī* – Blue *Saraswatī*	2nd Devi of Dasha Maha Vidya	174
63.	*Śrī Tripura Sundarī Devī*	3rd Devi of Dasha Maha Vidya	182
64.	ஸ்ரீ த்ரிபுர ஸுந்தரீ தேவீ	3rd Devi of Dasha Maha Vidya	192

#	Title	Remarks	Pages
65.	*Śrī Bhuvaneshwari Devī*	4th Devi of Dasha Maha Vidya	137
66.	ஸ்ரீ புவனேஸ்வரீ தேவீ	4th Devi of Dasha Maha Vidya	151
67.	*Śrī Tripura Bhairavi Devi*	5th Devi of Dasha Maha Vidya	132
68.	ஸ்ரீ த்ரிபுர பைரவீதேவீ	5th Devi of Dasha Maha Vidya	146
69.	*Śrī Kamalātmikā Devi*	6th Devi of Dasha Maha Vidya	138
70.	ஸ்ரீ சின்ன மஸ்தா தேவீ	6th Devi of Dasha Maha Vidya	164
71.	*Śrī Dhūmāvatī Devī*	7th Devi of Dasha Maha Vidya	141
72.	ஸ்ரீ தூமாவதீ தேவீ	7th Devi of Dasha Maha Vidya	166
73.	*Śrī Bhagalāmukhī Devī*	8th Devi of Dasha Maha Vidya	158
74.	ஸ்ரீ பகலாமுகீ தேவீ	8th Devi of Dasha Maha Vidya	186
75.	*Śrī Mātangī Devī*	9th Devi of Dasha Maha Vidya	145
76.	ஸ்ரீ மாதங்கீ3 தே3வீ	9th Devi of Dasha Maha Vidya	171
77.	*Śrī Kamalātmikā Devī*	10th Devi of Dasha Maha Vidya	170
78.	ஸ்ரீ கமலாத்மிகா தே3வீ	10th Devi of Dasha Maha Vidya	226
79.	*Chaṇḍī Homa Vidhānam*	Process of Performing Chandi Homam	60
80.	சண்டீ ஹோம விதானம்	Process of Performing Chandi Homam	80
81.	ஸ்ரீ ருத்3ர ந்யாசம் & த்ரிஶதீ	300 Divine names of Lord Rudra and Japa Nyasam	224
82.	*Śrī Rudra Nyāsa & Triśatī*	300 Divine names of Lord Rudra and Japa Nyasam	160
83.	ஸ்ரீ ஸூர்ய ஸஹஸ்ர நாமம்	கருத்துக்களுடன் ஒரு விளக்கம்	404
84.	*Śrī Sūrya Sahasranāmam*	Explanation with Comments	320
85.	Kalividambanam	An explanation	97
86.	கலிவிட³ம்ப³னம்	ஒரு விளக்கம்	100
87.	*Mūka Pancaśatī*	An Understanding	428
88.	மூக பஞ்ச ஶதி	ஒரு புரிதல்	577
89.	*Śrī Dattatreyar*	*Ādi Guru*	154
90.	ஸ்ரீ த³த்தாத்ரேயர்	ஆதி³ கு³ரு	174
	Applied Samskrutam Based		
91.	*Paribhāshā Stora–S*	An Exploration of *Lalitā Sahasranāmam*	96
92.	பரிபாஷா ஸ்தோத்ரங்கள்	ஸ்ரீ லலிதா ஸஹஸ்ரநாமம் - ஒரு ஆய்வு	135
93.	*Shrī Cakra*, An Esoteric Approach	Mathematical Construction to Draw *Shrī Cakra*	64
94.	ஸ்ரீ சக்கரம் வரையும் முறை	ஸ்ரீ சக்கரம் வரைய கணித கட்டுமானம்	84
95.	Number System in Samskrutam	An Overview of Mathematics Based on Samskrutam	123
96.	ஸமஸ்க்ருதத்தில் எண்ணியல்	ஸமஸ்க்ருதத்தில் பொதிந்துள்ள எண் கணிதம்	140
97.	*Vedic* Mathematics	30 Formulae Elucidated	146
98.	Vedic IT	Information Technology and Samskrutam	162

#	Title	Remarks	Pages
		IT Based	
99.	Orthogonal Array	A Statistical Tool for Software Testing	180
		Banking Based	
100.	Retail Banking	A Guide Book for Novice	213
101.	Corporate Banking	A Guide Book for Novice	232
102.	Dictionary of Financial Terms	A Guide Book for All – Demystifying Myriad Global Financial Terms	215
103.	GRC In BFS Industry	(**G**overnance, **R**isk Management and **C**ompliance by Banking & Finance Industry)	200

*****

www.ingramcontent.com/pod-product-compliance
Ingram Content Group UK Ltd.
Pitfield, Milton Keynes, MK11 3LW, UK
UKHW011513190726
13845UKWH00034B/1241

9 789334 278491